Cabinets & Shelves

L ike almost all furnishings, shelves and cabinets serve very practical purposes. But they also exert a powerful decorating influence. One reason, of course, is sheer size: Constructed on a wall, these elements frequently exceed in height and width adjacent doors or windows, and freestanding shelves and cabinets, because of their dimensions, often lord it over other pieces of furniture in a room. Another reason for their decorative effect is what they hold. Since they frequently display your favorite treasures, even small-sized cabinets or shelves become natural attention-grabbers. Filled with books, they make a quieter but nonetheless impressive statement.

You can exploit these attributes to create or emphasize any of a variety of room designs. For example, you can position a freestanding shelf unit to divide a large space or to channel traffic flow between two areas. Depending on how much separation you want, the storage unit can either be open, with widely spaced shelves that afford considerable visibility through the structure, or have a solid back that serves as a sight barrier. You can also use a shelf-and-cabinet system to rationalize a wall that has an embarrassment of niches and openings, superimposing order along with the new units.

Whatever your purpose, plan your design carefully. Shelving and cabinetry should complement the rest of the furnishings. Satin-finished steel works most happily in a room where other materials are equally streamlined; painted or stained woods with unobtrusive support hardware blend willingly with traditional, conservatively furnished interiors. And consider scale — in relation to the other furnishings, to the objects to be displayed, and to the room as a whole — keeping the visual weight of shelves and cabinets in proportion to their surroundings.

The photographic prologue on the following pages provides a sampling of designs that are notably successful in each of these particulars. In the text and illustrations that begin on page 16, you will become familiar with the basic materials of shelving and cabinetry and proceed step by step through the assembly of projects that will do you equally proud.

Wrap-around shelving brings a high-ceilinged room down to cozy proportions *(above)*. The lowest shelf is set at the level of the raised fireplace hearth; another shelf serves in part as a mantelpiece. Adjustable ceiling lights spotlight the owner's flock of old shorebird decoys, marching smartly across the top shelf.

Tiers of shelving, engineered with no visible means of support, hold a small fleet of nautical memorabilia in the study at left. Locating the shelves on either side of the fireplace, a natural focal point, assures the collection the attention it deserves.

Wedded to the room as part of its basic architecture, the handsome bookcases and cabinets at left appear to be built into the wall behind them. The unit is paneled with poplar and framed by vertical strips of ash; both are finished with a clear varnish. The same hardwoods run across the ceiling, the rays of lighter-toned ash drawing the eye toward a door that opens onto the garden beyond. The desk and shelves on the adjoining wall, though they employ the same woods and same proportions, project out from the wall to vary the effect. In both instances, cabinet, shelf and drawer hardware is concealed, so that all of the wood surfaces are uniformly sleek.

Roof support, room divider and shelving all in one, the massive framework above is an integral part of the house's structure. Because the shelf unit stands where floor levels change, it also marks the location of the stairs. Vertical load-bearing members are plaster sheathed, just as the walls and ceiling are. The shelves, too, have been plastered, the lowermost being overlaid with a highly polished deck of mahogany. Bathed in natural light, the shelf divider provides brilliant display for decorative glassware.

A handsome interplay of lines, angles, surfaces and solids, the wall unit at left is as much an exercise in decorative geometry as in storage. Slender steel uprights rise from the floor and bend inward to the wall at top to support the shelves along their front edges. Additional support is supplied by fasteners that go through shelf backsplashes into the wall behind.

Slotted standards, knife brackets and
glass shelving are the ready-made elements
combined in this assembly. Putting molding around the niche that holds the shelves
and installing a storage cabinet below has
yielded an important-looking showcase for a
collection of Aztec and Maya artifacts.
And because the shelves are transparent,
room light is able to wash every corner
of the display surface.

The space where a window once existed
in this farmhouse has been transformed into
shelving complemented by an antique
cupboard just tall enough to fit beneath. To
make the joining neater, the cabinet has
been given a new top and its old turquoise-
colored buttermilk paint echoed in the
woodwork around the room.

A harmonious composition of doors, drawers and shelves, based on a single module with many variations, fills one entire wall of this sleek room. The same principle o.

modulation is used in the color scheme — which runs in five measured steps from glossy white to glossy black.

Other Publications:
UNDERSTANDING COMPUTERS
THE ENCHANTED WORLD
THE KODAK LIBRARY OF CREATIVE PHOTOGRAPHY
GREAT MEALS IN MINUTES
THE CIVIL WAR
PLANET EARTH
COLLECTOR'S LIBRARY OF THE CIVIL WAR
THE EPIC OF FLIGHT
THE GOOD COOK
THE SEAFARERS
WORLD WAR II
HOME REPAIR AND IMPROVEMENT
THE OLD WEST

For information on and a full
description of any of the Time-Life Books
series listed above, please write:
Reader Information
Time-Life Books
541 North Fairbanks Court
Chicago, Illinois 60611

This volume is one of a series that features home decorating projects.

Cabinets & Shelves

by the Editors of Time-Life Books

TIME-LIFE BOOKS □ ALEXANDRIA, VIRGINIA

YOUR HOME

SERIES DIRECTOR: Gerry Schremp
Deputy Director: Adrian Allen
Deputy Director for Text: Jim Hicks
Designer: Susan K. White
Series Administrator: Loretta Y. Britten
Editorial Staff for *Cabinets & Shelves*
Text Editors: John Newton, Lydia Preston
Staff Writers: Allan Fallow, Kathleen M. Kiely,
Glenn Martin McNatt, Jane A. Martin
Copy Coordinator: Robert M. S. Somerville
Art Assistant: Jennifer B. Gilman
Picture Coordinator: Renée DeSandies
Editorial Assistant: Carolyn Wall Rothery

Special Contributors: Anne Cleveland Kalicki,
Leslie Marshall, Wendy Buehr Murphy,
Jonathan Walters

Editorial Operations
Design: Ellen Robling (assistant director)
Copy Chief: Diane Ullius
Editorial Operations: Caroline A. Boubin
(manager)
Production: Celia Beattie
Quality Control: James J. Cox (director),
Sally Collins
Library: Louise D. Forstall

Correspondents: Elisabeth Kraemer-Singh
(Bonn); Margot Hapgood, Dorothy Bacon
(London); Miriam Hsia (New York); Maria
Vincenza Aloisi, Josephine du Brusle (Paris);
Ann Natanson (Rome). Valuable assistance was
also provided by: Carolyn T. Chubet (New York).

THE CONSULTANT

Frederick L. Wall, a furniture maker and sculptor,
is an instructor in furniture design at the Corcoran
School of Art in Washington, D.C. His work has
been featured in many exhibits and publications.
Mr. Wall is responsible for designing and building
many of the projects shown in this volume.

© 1985 Time-Life Books Inc. All rights reserved.
No part of this book may be reproduced in any
form or by any electronic or mechanical means,
including information storage and retrieval devices
or systems, without prior written permission from
the publisher, except that brief passages may be
quoted for reviews.

First printing. Printed in U.S.A.

Published simultaneously in Canada.
School and library distribution by Silver Burdett
Company, Morristown, New Jersey 07960.

TIME-LIFE is a trademark of
Time Incorporated U.S.A.

Library of Congress Cataloguing in
Publication Data
Main entry under title:
Cabinets & shelves.

(Your home)
Includes index.
1. Cabinet-work. 2. Shelving (Furniture).
I. Time-Life Books. II. Title: Cabinets and shelves.
III. Series: Your home (Alexandria, Va.)
TT197.C22 1985   684.1'6   85-12621
ISBN 0-8094-5516-1
ISBN 0-8094-5517-X (lib. bdg.)

CONTENTS

The wondrous versatility of wood

Nothing nature produces makes a more versatile or pleasing construction material than wood. Beautiful to look at, warm to the touch, responsive to cutting and shaping, it can also be remarkably strong, durable and easy to care for. But beyond these general qualities are significant differences among wood species: Color, grain, density, stability, weight and certainly cost vary with each kind of wood or wood product. The success of any project will depend in large measure on how much you know about woods, how skilled you are in selecting the right grades and cuts, and how sharp your eye is in detecting defects in individual boards.

As the chart opposite shows, board lumber is divided into softwood and hardwood. The two terms have more to do with the way trees grow and their cellular alignment or graining than with softness or hardness. Softwoods are the products of needle-bearing evergreens, such as firs and pines, and are typically straight-grained, light-colored and rather uniform in appearance. They are ideal for shelving and for framing cabinets because they combine strength and lightness with relative low cost and wide availability.

The softwood lumber industry markets boards in lengths ranging from 8 to 20 feet. Standard thicknesses and widths start at 1-by-2 and rise to 2-by-12. But these are nominal rather than actual sizes. The dimensions exist only at the moment the green boards leave the rough-cutting mill. Trimming, squaring, dressing and drying reduce the width and thickness of boards by nearly 25 per cent, so that a 2-by-4 at the lumberyard is actually 1½ by 3½ inches.

Depending upon the natural growth characteristics of a given tree, the part of a tree that a board is cut from and the manufacturing process used to dress it, lumber will vary considerably in quality. To account for these differences, each sector of the industry follows a detailed grading system. For softwood, the kinds and frequencies of imperfections, including knotholes, checks, pitch streaks, torn grain and machine burns, are toted up and the board lumber rated as either Select or Common. Selects include subgrades of premium, clear and nearly clear wood — all kiln-dried to 15 per cent or less moisture content and suitable for cabinets or shelving. Less costly Commons are too marred and too unstable.

Grading generally provides a good guide to getting the quality you want, but keep in mind that boards can warp and twist after they reach the lumberyard. Shop at a reputable dealer who cares for the stock well. When buying materials for any project, inspect each board for straightness. You can do this by sighting along each of the four sides; if you detect a curve along any plane, ask for another board. Dimensions demand to be double-checked with a ruler — especially if the boards must match.

Hardwoods are produced by broad-leaved trees, including native oak and tropical mahogany to name some prized examples. They are characterized by more highly figured and complex graining than softwoods, as well as a greater range of colors. Hardwoods are invariably more expensive than softwoods, but they are preferred where fine appearance and durability are prime considerations.

Hardwood lumber is usually sold in random lengths and widths; the most common thickness of rough boards is 1 inch, which the industry expresses as 4/4. When smooth-finished — or dressed — on both the front and back, the boards are identified as S2S and are $^{13}/_{16}$ inch thick.

Hardwoods are graded within each species as Firsts and Seconds — the finest of lumber — followed by Selects; any of these may be used for cabinetry and finished with a transparent coating. Hardwood Commons Nos. 1 and 2 are adequate for cabinets and shelving that will be enameled.

Plywoods suitable for interior use are typically constructed of three to nine cross-laminated layers of wood, with one or both faces smooth-finished and the remainder rough core wood. More warp-resistant than lumber of comparable thickness, they come in softwood and hardwood types, the classification derived from the kind of wood veneer used to face the plywood sheets. Their sizes vary but panels are most commonly 4 feet by 8 feet, in thicknesses ranging from ⅛ to 1 inch.

Each face is graded separately — from A to D in softwood, from A to 4 in hardwood. Softwood plywood graded AA or AB interior and ¼ inch thick is an excellent choice for cabinet backs and bottoms; ¾-inch thickness serves for shelving. Hardwood plywoods are considerably less expensive and lighter in weight than hardwood boards. And hardwood plywoods faced with veneers cut from a crotch, burl or stump offer rich figuring that would not be possible with conventionally sawed lumber. Other board products — particleboard and hardboard — are less strong than either lumber or plywood, but can be used as cabinet backing or as rough shelving where spans are short and support requirements modest.

A Solid Slab

SOFTWOOD BOARDS

Woods   Pine, spruce, fir, cedar, larch.

Sizes   Thicknesses nominally 1 or 2 inches, actually ¾ or 1½ inches; widths nominally 2 to 12 inches, actually 1½ to 11¼ inches; lengths from 8 to 20 feet in 2-foot increments.

Grades   Select, or Clear, subdivided into A (no knots or splits), B (a few blemishes), C (a few small tight knots) and D (numerous small knots); Common, subdivided into Nos. 1 through 5, with increasingly large, numerous, loose knots (only 1 and 2 are suitable for shelves).

HARDWOOD BOARDS

Woods   Dozens, including ash, cherry, oak, maple, walnut, mahogany, rosewood, teak.

Sizes   Thickness of 13/16 inch, smooth on face and back, is most common; widths and lengths are random.

Grades   Firsts and Seconds (no knots or splits); Selects (no knots or splits on face, small defects on back); Commons No. 1 and No. 2 have some knots and splits but can be painted.

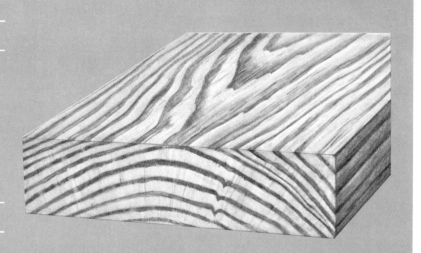

Boards are sawed lengthwise from the tree's trunk, so the grain, or pattern, in their faces and sides reveals the long tubular cells of which wood is composed. The ends of boards show the tubes' cut ends; these are naturally more porous than the sides or faces and less secure as anchorage for screws and other fasteners.

A Wood Sandwich

SOFTWOOD PLYWOOD

Woods   Fir, pine, larch, hemlock, spruce, cedar, redwood.

Sizes   Thickness varies with plies — three-ply: ¼, 5/16, ⅜ inch; five-ply: ½, ⅝, ¾ inch; seven-ply: ⅞ to 1⅛ inches. Standard panels are 4 by 8 feet; on special order, widths range from 2 to 5 feet, lengths up to 16 feet.

Grades   A has minor defects and patches; B, C and D have successively more defects; N — available on special order — is virtually defect-free.

HARDWOOD PLYWOOD

Woods   Face plies commonly cherry, oak, birch, black walnut, maple, mahogany, teak. Interior may be hardwood or softwood, veneers or lumber, or particleboard.

Sizes   Thickness varies with plies — three-ply: ⅛, 3/16, ¼ inch; five-ply: ¼, ⅜, ½, ⅝ inch; seven-ply: ⅝, ¾ inch; nine-ply: ¾, 1 inch. Standard panels are 4 by 8 feet; other sizes are available on special order.

Grades   A — face veneer has matched joints and grains; B — face fairly well matched; 2 — veneers on face do not match, no open defects allowed; 3 — tight knots, slight defects; 4 — larger defects.

Plywood is made up of an odd number of layers, or plies, of wood held together by adhesive but shown peeled back here. The layers may all be thin veneer, or the outer layers may be thin and the inner layers of thicker wood or particleboard. The grain of alternate layers is always at right angles, but the grain of the two outside layers must be parallel to provide stability.

Shelves: Easy, ornamental and always useful

Few of the fixtures or furnishings you can build for your home offer a more rewarding return on investment than shelves. It is axiomatic that a home cannot have too many shelves. Compared with other do-it-yourself projects, they are relatively easy to construct and usually cost far less than comparable ready-made units. And best of all, by building them yourself, you can be sure they are expressly designed for your space, your décor and the use that you plan to make of them—virtues that might cost a small fortune if provided instead by a cabinetmaker.

The first step in planning shelves is to answer some questions. What will you put on them? Do you want them for storage or display, or a combination of both? Do you want them to be fixed or movable? Against a wall or elsewhere in a room?

The answers will guide you in determining the type and size of shelves to construct. If they are to hold books, for instance, shelves should be at least 8 inches deep and have 9 inches of clearance for volumes of average size; they should be 12 inches deep with 13 inches of clearance for larger books. (It will also help to know that you can fit eight to 10 books of average size on each running foot of shelf.) If instead you want to show off a particular collection of *objets,* you can lay the items on their sides on a large sheet of paper, arrange them in an eye-pleasing fashion, then trace their outlines and plan the shelves to fit that pattern.

Some shelves are exceptionally easy to create. And ease of construction need not equate with crudeness of appearance, as the handsome units opposite prove. Once the boards are sawed to size and finished, assembling the set of shelves in the upper drawing is virtually child's play, involving nothing more than nailing the metal joint clips into place. The lower unit is only marginally more difficult; the angle irons that hold it together are fastened with screws, requiring you to drill pilot holes.

Units like these—or any cupboard or other frame with two vertical sides facing each other—can be equipped with adjustable shelves by adding commercially available metal tracks and bracket clips that support the shelves from the ends *(page 20).* Another type of slotted track or standard fitted with large brackets *(pages 22-23)* offers a ready way to hang utilitarian shelving on a wall.

Your shelf-making repertoire can easily encompass works of greater elegance, however, and without hard-to-acquire skills or special tools. By turning standards and brackets toward the wall and concealing them behind wood posts, for example, you can transform the above-mentioned utilitarian system into an eye-catching unit of stylish simplicity *(pages 38-43).* With a more substantial investment of time and effort—but again, without special skills—you can create a fine, freestanding bookcase in the traditional style *(pages 28-33)* or even cover an entire wall with a classic set of shelves surrounding a window *(pages 60-67).*

Several of the shelf projects that follow—and others you might design yourself—need to be anchored to walls. The most secure anchorages are studs, vertical wood framing members found behind wallboard in most modern houses. Instructions for locating studs are on page 21. Appropriate fasteners for use in studs, in wallboard where studs are not available, and in other kinds of walls are described on page 125.

Quick Assembly with Joint Clips and Corner Braces

Special hardware makes assembling these shelf units as easy as piecing together a child's oversized puzzle. Most of the work is in cutting and finishing the boards. They then can be quickly fastened together, either with the joint clips (called corner clips by the manufacturer) in the top drawing, or with the angle irons — corner braces — in the bottom picture.

The brass-plated clips are made in two sizes: ¾ inch for nominal 1-inch softwood boards and ⅝ inch for laminated particleboard. They come in L shapes, T shapes and crosses.

First draw a plan for the shelves — either full size or to scale. Double-check that parallel distances correspond correctly — for instance, that the board lengths and thicknesses of measurement AA (top) total the same as those for measurement BB.

Whether the boards are sawed by you or the lumberyard, make sure the cuts are square. Assemble the boards without nails first, to check for fit, then sand and finish them before reassembly: They can be stained and oiled, enameled, varnished or even covered with fabric held by staples. When figuring how many of each clip to buy, remember those for the rear side of the unit. Fasten the clips with 16-gauge round-head brass pins, ¾ inch long. Drive the pins through the small holes on the front, not the larger ones on the sides, which result from the manufacturing process.

Small angle irons — these have 1½-inch legs — offer another way to hold shelves together. If using nominal 1-inch boards, fasten the irons with ¾-inch No. 6 flat-head wood screws, driven into 1/16-inch-wide pilot holes. Make sure screws driven from opposite sides of a board will not collide, and assemble the pieces in such an order that boards fixed in place leave you room to drill holes and drive screws for later boards. Angle irons do not provide much rigidity, so you may wish to nail a ¼-inch plywood back on your unit for added stability.

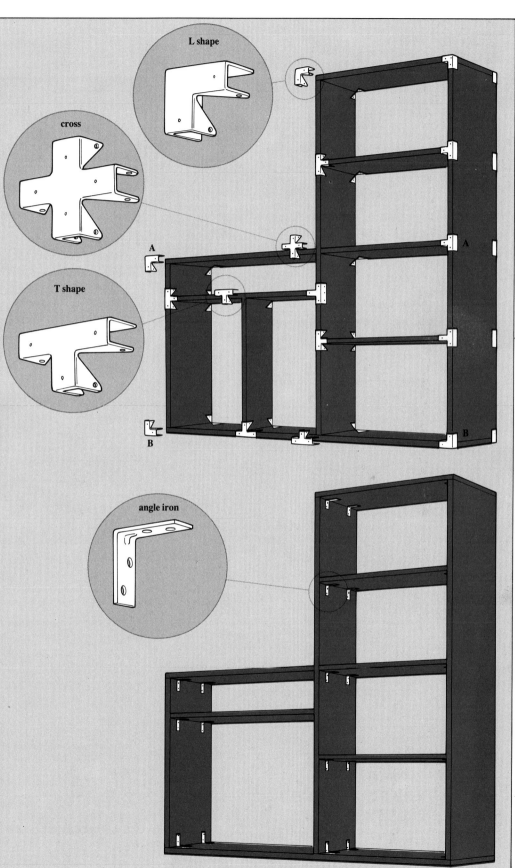

L shape

cross

T shape

A

B

A

B

angle iron

Movable Clips for Adjustable Shelves

You can install adjustable shelves in units like those on the preceding page, or anywhere else where two facing vertical surfaces form a frame. The shelves rest on movable bracket clips that fit into horizontal slots in vertical metal tracks.

The tracks come in lengths ranging from 12 inches to 12 feet and can be cut to exact size with a hacksaw (but be sure to cut the same amount from the same ends of tracks that must match for level shelves). They can be attached to the surface, as shown here, or they can be recessed in dadoes — channels carved in the wood with a router *(page 87, Step 3)*. Setting the tracks into dadoes improves the unit's appearance, since there will be no sizable gaps between the ends of the shelves and the side walls. Another way to eliminate the gaps is to notch the ends of the shelf boards with a saber saw so they will fit around the tracks *(lower drawing)*. Whether in dadoes or on the surface, the tracks must be mounted plumb and exactly level with each other *(page 22, Steps 2 and 3)*.

The upper shelf here is supported on a form of flattened brackets known as flush clips; heavy loads need stronger, triangular gusset clips *(top right)*. Squeeze flush or gusset clips with pliers to compress them enough to get them into their slots.

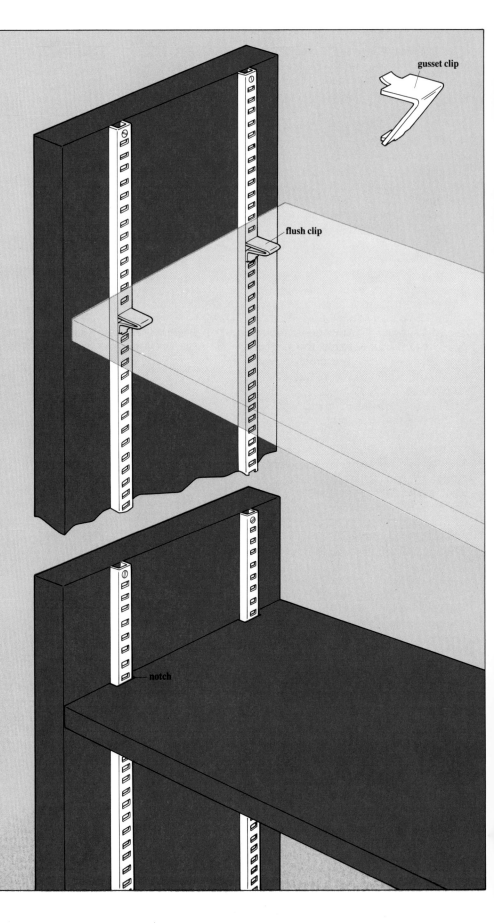

gusset clip

flush clip

notch

Finding Safe Anchorage

The 2-by-4 wood studs behind the wallboard of most modern houses are ideal supports for shelves that need to be fixed to walls. Techniques for locating these framing members are almost as numerous as the studs themselves.

Experienced carpenters rely on ear and eye: Rapping on a wall, they listen for the change from a hollow to a dull, solid sound that indicates the presence of a stud. Or, shining a flashlight along the wall, they look for slight mounds and cracks in the paint that develop as wallboard nails loosen over the years.

Some stores sell electronic stud finders and magnetic stud finders, which respond respectively to density of material and to metal. While the electronic ones are fairly dependable, the magnetic ones react to pipes and electric wiring just as they do to nails in studs and are therefore often misleading.

The technique shown here involves drilling a tiny hole in the wall (which can be easily filled with spackling compound) and probing with a wire to learn the location of a stud. Because studs are usually at 16-inch intervals — measuring from the center of one to the center of the next — you can often plot the positions of others without drilling, once you have located one. Check by driving a nail where the adjacent stud should be.

There are exceptions. In houses built before World War II, studs may be at other intervals. In homes built since 1970, the studs of interior partition walls — and, less often, exterior walls — are sometimes set at 24-inch intervals.

If you wish to fasten a shelving framework to the ceiling, this same method can be used to find joists, the overhead framing members. Wear safety goggles when drilling overhead.

Caution: When drilling, beware of pipes and electric cables. Look for plumbing and electric outlets on both sides of a wall. Cables are usually found near floors and adjacent to doors. If you feel the bit hit metal, stop drilling. If you think you have damaged plumbing or electric lines, call a professional.

1 Drilling through the wall. Find the approximate location of a hidden stud by rapping lightly along the wall with your knuckles and listening for a solid, as opposed to a hollow, sound. A few inches away, drill a small hole angled sharply toward the suspected stud location (*above*).

2 Probing with wire. Feed a thin, stiff wire into the angled hole until the tip of the wire encounters solid resistance. (You may have to push through insulation, which offers cushiony resistance.) Grasp the wire at the hole between thumb and forefinger and extract it. Hold the wire outside the wall at the same position and angle as when it was in the hole. Its tip should indicate the side of the stud; mark that place on the wall.

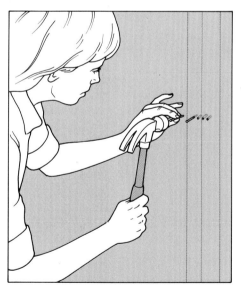

3 Proving the edges of the stud. To confirm the stud's location, measure ¾ inch beyond the mark and drive a nail through the wallboard until you feel it enter wood. Then drive nails ¾ inch to both sides of that place, moving them minute distances and driving them again until you establish exactly where the right and left edges of the stud are (*above*). Mark the midpoint between the edges to indicate the stud's center.

4 Marking the center line of the stud. Hold a carpenter's level vertically against the wall so that one edge is aligned with the marked center of the stud. When the bubbles in the top and bottom windows of the level are centered, use the level as a straightedge to draw a vertical line down the center of the stud.

Basic Tracks and Brackets

Wall standards that hold adjustable shelf-support brackets come in many lengths, and brackets are made to hold shelves with a front-to-back measurement from 6 inches up to 2 feet. These steps show how to mount the most common type — single-slotted standards with knife brackets. Others, like those opposite, are installed in much the same way.

A shelf should extend about 4 to 8 inches beyond each end support — far enough not to slip off the bracket if the shelf is bumped, but not so far that loads placed outside the bracket will tip the shelf. Some brackets (*opposite, top*) can be fixed to shelves with screws to prevent slipping and tipping.

Whenever possible, anchor the standards to studs (*page 21*). If stud locations are inconvenient, or if you have masonry walls, see page 125 to find the appropriate fastener. Be wary, however, of putting heavy loads on standards fastened to wallboard. Be sure to position standards top end up; some are oriented to work in one direction only.

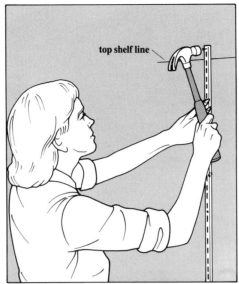

1 **Positioning the end standards.** Sketch a level line lightly across the wall to mark the approximate height and length of your top shelf. Plot and mark positions for the end, or outermost, standards so that the shelves will extend an equal distance beyond each of them. Secure one end standard temporarily in place at its marked position by driving a small nail through the mounting hole at its top (*above*), letting its lower end hang free.

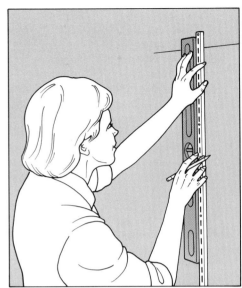

2 **Plumbing the first standard.** Holding a carpenter's level against the wall alongside the standard, adjust the position of the standard until the bubbles in the top and bottom windows indicate it is vertical, or plumb. With a pencil, mark the location of the standard's mounting holes on the wall. Then remove the standard and drill the holes you will need for the correct fasteners (*page 125*) at all the marked locations. Attach the standard.

3 **Leveling the second end standard.** Position a long, straight board so that one end rests on top of the already-mounted standard and the other end crosses the marked position for the other end standard. Have a helper hold the board and a carpenter's level atop it. When the board is level, hold the second end standard at its marked location with its top butting against the board. Make a pencil mark through the top mounting hole, remove the board and level, and drive a small nail through the hole. Then plumb this standard and mount it with fasteners (*Step 2*).

4 **Inserting brackets.** Mount any intervening standards. Insert a bracket for the top shelf in an end standard and drive it into the slots by hammering lightly on a wood block held on top of it. Count slots from the top of the standard or from a mounting screw to find the matching slots on the other standards. Install those brackets, then check with the board and level to be sure the brackets are at the same level. Now install the brackets for other shelves.

A Quartet of Options

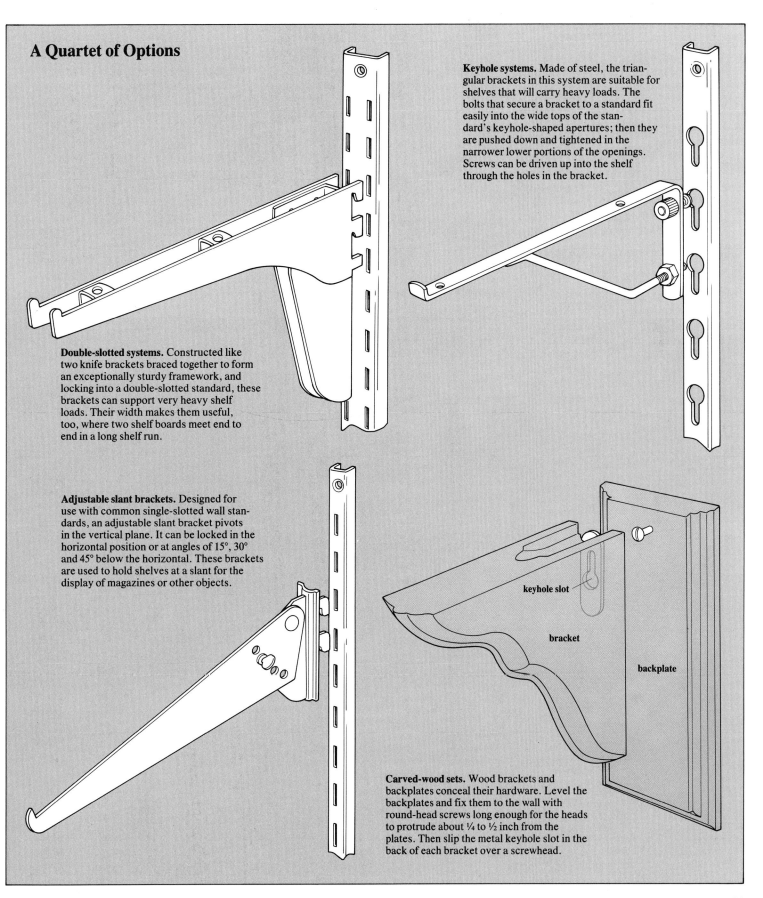

Keyhole systems. Made of steel, the triangular brackets in this system are suitable for shelves that will carry heavy loads. The bolts that secure a bracket to a standard fit easily into the wide tops of the standard's keyhole-shaped apertures; then they are pushed down and tightened in the narrower lower portions of the openings. Screws can be driven up into the shelf through the holes in the bracket.

Double-slotted systems. Constructed like two knife brackets braced together to form an exceptionally sturdy framework, and locking into a double-slotted standard, these brackets can support very heavy shelf loads. Their width makes them useful, too, where two shelf boards meet end to end in a long shelf run.

Adjustable slant brackets. Designed for use with common single-slotted wall standards, an adjustable slant bracket pivots in the vertical plane. It can be locked in the horizontal position or at angles of 15°, 30° and 45° below the horizontal. These brackets are used to hold shelves at a slant for the display of magazines or other objects.

keyhole slot

bracket

backplate

Carved-wood sets. Wood brackets and backplates conceal their hardware. Level the backplates and fix them to the wall with round-head screws long enough for the heads to protrude about ¼ to ½ inch from the plates. Then slip the metal keyhole slot in the back of each bracket over a screwhead.

23

A shelf on sturdy brackets

Wood-bracket shelves mounted directly into wall studs are the simplest shelving to construct — and among the most attractive. Sturdy shelves like those shown below, built of solid pine and finished to emphasize the wood's grain, complement contemporary furnishings as well as rustic 18th Century styles.

Birch dowels plugging the screw holes stand out dark against the pine; the trio of plugs on the shelf cleat are manifest evidence that the shelves are hand-crafted. Centering the shelves on studs, as here, ensures that the plugs are symmetrical.

All of the components for one of these shelves can be cut from a single 8-foot length of nominal ⁵⁄₄-by-12 pine board or more common 1-by-12. (The finished sizes of the boards are 1 by 11½ inches and ¾ by 11½ inches.) Have your lumber dealer cut off two 1-foot-long pieces from the end of each board and rip-cut a 2-inch-wide strip from the remaining 6-foot length. Use the broad 6-foot piece for the shelf; the narrow strip will form the cleat. Cut the curved brackets out of the two 1-foot-long pieces with a saber saw. The dowel plugs can be cut at home with a backsaw and miter box or purchased ready-made from a hardware store.

To tailor the shelves to your special needs, you can reduce their overall length to as little as 36 inches or — providing you use an additional bracket every 4 feet — you can extend them to 12 feet. The brackets can be shaped more fancifully to a design of your own; just keep the length of each leg the same as in the pattern shown at right and be sure that no part of the design is too narrow to support the load — a width of 1 inch is minimum.

Only a few basic tools are required to assemble the shelf. In addition to a screwdriver, a pair of C clamps, a carpenter's level and a saber saw, you will also need a variable-speed power drill with ⅜-inch and ³⁄₁₆-inch twist bits.

After you assemble the pieces and fill in the screw holes on the top of the shelf with plugs, smooth all surfaces with medium (100-grit) sandpaper, and brush on several coats of a clear penetrating oil finish. Mount the shelf on the wall, then cover the three screw holes in the mounting cleat with dowel plugs, and sand and finish them as described above.

Materials List (for one shelf)

⁵⁄₄ x 12	8 ′ yellow pine ⁵⁄₄ x 12, cut into: 2 pieces, 1 ′ long 1 piece, 6 ′ long, ripped lengthwise into 1 piece 9½ ″ wide and 1 piece 2 ″ wide
Dowel plugs	1 package ⅜ ″ birch dowel plugs
Screws	15 No. 10 flat-head wood screws, 2 ″ long

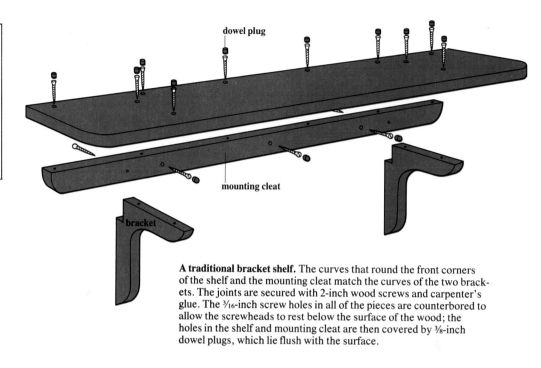

dowel plug

mounting cleat

bracket

A traditional bracket shelf. The curves that round the front corners of the shelf and the mounting cleat match the curves of the two brackets. The joints are secured with 2-inch wood screws and carpenter's glue. The ³⁄₁₆-inch screw holes in all of the pieces are counterbored to allow the screwheads to rest below the surface of the wood; the holes in the shelf and mounting cleat are then covered by ⅜-inch dowel plugs, which lie flush with the surface.

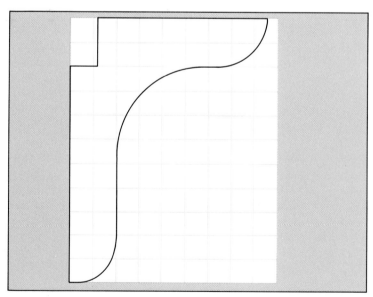

1 **Making the bracket pattern.** Draw a grid of 1-inch squares on a 9-by-11-inch piece of lightweight cardboard or heavy paper. Using the pattern above as a guide, draw a rectangular notch in one corner of the grid. Then mark the points where the outline of the front edge of the bracket crosses the grid and connect the marks with smooth curves. Cut out the pattern with scissors.

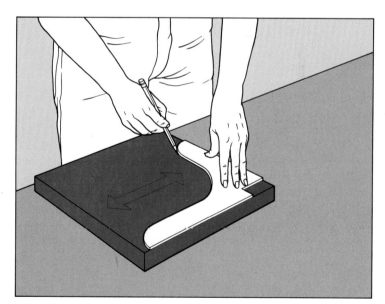

2 **Transferring the pattern to wood.** Position the bracket pattern on one of the 1-foot pieces of wood, making sure the upward sweep of the pattern runs in the same direction as the wood's grain. Trace around the pattern with a pencil. Then transfer the pattern to the second 1-foot wood piece in the same way. ▶

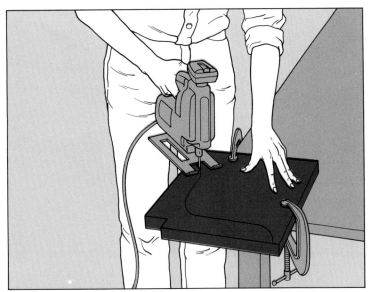

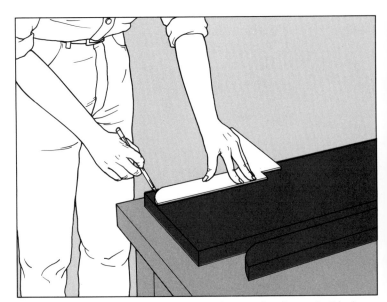

3 **Cutting the brackets.** Position one bracket piece on a work surface with the rectangular notch of the traced pattern overhanging the edge. Clamp the board in place and use a saber saw outfitted with a medium woodcutting blade to cut out the notch. Move the piece outward so the curved pattern overhangs the work surface. Clamp the board again and cut out the bracket (*above*). Clamp and cut the second bracket in the same way. Finally, smooth the curves of the brackets with a sanding block wrapped in coarse (60-grit) sandpaper.

4 **Rounding shelf and cleat corners.** Lay the mounting cleat on its 2-inch side. Pencil a mark 2 inches from each end. Place the bracket pattern on the cleat, aligning one straight outside edge of the pattern with one side edge of the cleat. Set the tip of the curved end at the mark. Then trace the curve onto the wood. Repeat at the other end of the cleat, turning the pattern over so both curves in the cleat will be on the same side. Clamp the piece to the work surface and cut rounded corners at each end of the cleat with a saber saw. Finally, trace the curve onto one edge of each end of the shelf, aligning the straight inside edge of the pattern with the shelf edge (*above*). Saw off those shelf corners, then smooth all of the edges of both pieces with coarse (60-grit) sandpaper.

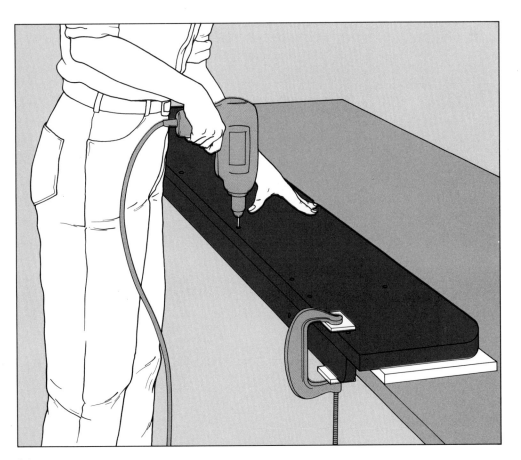

7 **Joining the shelf and cleat.** Set the shelf at one edge of the work surface on top of scrap wood. Align the cleat against the bottom surface of the shelf so that the back edge of the shelf is flush with the back edge of the cleat (the back of the cleat is the side with only 2 counterbored holes); the shelf should overhang the cleat by 2 inches at each end. Clamp the pieces together at both ends.

Use a drill with a $\frac{3}{16}$-inch twist bit to drill pilot holes in the top of the cleat through the holes along the back of the shelf (*left*).

Unclamp the pieces and apply yellow carpenter's glue to the top surface of the cleat. Clamp the pieces back together and secure the joint with 2-inch No. 10 screws. Remove the clamps.

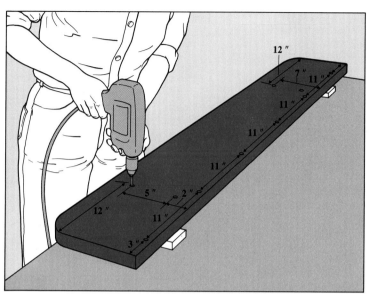

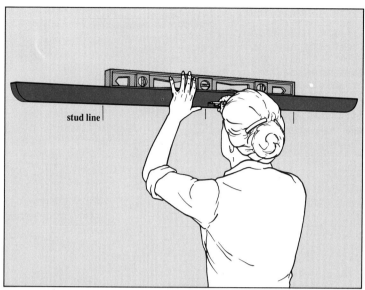

5 **Starting counterbored screw holes.** Draw a very light pencil line ½ inch from and parallel to the shelf's long edge on the side opposite the rounded corners. Mark across the line 3 inches from each end and at 11-inch intervals in between. Then draw pencil lines across the width of the board 12 inches from each end, and make marks 2 inches and 7 inches from the marked long edge. Raise the shelf from the work surface with scraps of wood. Wrap a piece of tape around a ⅜-inch twist bit ½ inch from the tip to gauge the depth of the hole. Fit the bit into a variable-speed drill and bore ½-inch-deep holes at each mark. Then use a ³⁄₁₆-inch bit to bore all the way through the wood at each hole.

6 **Leveling the cleat.** Measure 10 inches from each end of the cleat, and mark the center of its broad face. Then use a yardstick and pencil to draw a light line about 3 feet long across the wall where you want the shelf. Find the studs behind this section of wall *(page 21)* and mark them with vertical lines. Hold the cleat against the wall so its top edge is flush with the shelf line and the marked side faces the wall. Center it on stud lines if you can, level it, then mark the stud lines on the cleat *(above)*. Set the cleat atop wood scraps on a work surface and mark the center of the face at each stud line. Drill ½-inch holes at the marks with a ⅜-inch twist bit, then drill through the holes with a ³⁄₁₆-inch bit. Turn the cleat over and drill similar holes at the two marks on the other side.

8 **Attaching the mounting brackets.** Clamp the shelf face down at the edge of the work surface. Align the center of the notch in one bracket with the holes in the mounting cleat and shelf. Use a drill fitted with a ³⁄₁₆-inch twist bit to drill a pilot hole through the hole in the cleat into the back edge of the bracket *(right)*, and secure the joint with a 2-inch No. 10 screw.

Turn the shelf right side up and drill pilot holes similarly in the top edge of the bracket through the holes in the shelf, and secure with screws. Then disassemble the pieces, apply glue to the edges of the notch and top of the bracket, and reattach to the shelf with screws.

Attach the other end bracket to the shelf with glue and screws the same way. Mount the shelf as described in the text.

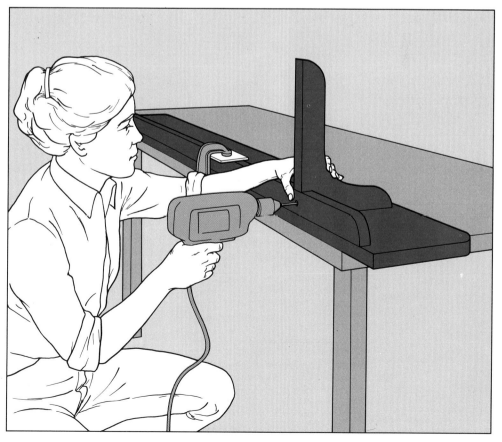

Simplified joinery for a handsome bookcase

Following in the proud tradition of 19th Century farmhouse furniture, the pine bookcase below bespeaks an unpretentious elegance. Its construction represents a simplified version of cabinetwork techniques — the frame is nailed rather than screwed, for example — so even a novice can reproduce it.

The simplicity of the construction also dictates the use of softwoods — pine, fir, spruce and the like — which are readily available in nominal 1-inch boards of various widths. Clear, finish-grade wood, free of defects, is essential if the bookcase is to be stained; otherwise, a grade of slightly lesser quality will serve.

The bookcase here is 36¾ inches high, 46 inches wide and 11¼ inches deep overall; its shelves are 41¾ and 42 inches wide. You can decrease these measurements to produce a smaller piece, but the design does not lend itself to enlarging them: Shelves longer than 42 inches tend to sag under a full load of books.

If you like, you can saw the boards to length, ripping three to width, as specified in the Materials List. Or have the wood sawed at the lumberyard, by a dealer who specializes in providing the precise cutting demanded by cabinetmakers.

In any case, you will have to saw certain small pieces of molding and other trim to fit as you construct the bookcase. Molding comes in a variety of shapes with picturesque names; this bookcase features ogee cap molding around the base and bed molding around the top. The backstops, which hold the back panel in place, are made of ½-inch-by-¾-inch wood strips called parting bead.

If you choose different molding styles

from those shown here, be sure their dimensions fit the proportions of the bookcase. Buy stain-grade molding with no joints if you plan to apply a clear finish. Finger-jointed molding, somewhat cheaper, is suitable for enameling.

Building the bookcase calls for the basic tools: claw hammer, measuring tape, drill and crosscut saw or backsaw. Two more-specialized tools help you achieve professional-looking results: A miter box *(Step 8)* guides the saw for making perfect 45° or 90° cuts; a nail set *(Step 11)* keeps hammer blows from bruising fancy moldings and sinks nailheads slightly below the wood's surface. Finally, a homemade jig *(Step 7)* guides you in drilling symmetrical rows of holes for the bracket pins that support adjustable shelves.

When the bookcase is assembled, fill holes, cracks and depressions with wood putty. Use fine (150-grit) sandpaper to smooth the dried putty, rough edges and the cut ends of boards; take care not to abrade the molding detail. Finish the bookcase with stain and varnish or shellac, or with an oil- or latex-based enamel.

Materials List

Pine lumber	46 " clear pine 1 x 12
	17 ' clear pine 1 x 10, cut into:
	2 side panels, 36 " long
	1 bottom shelf, 42 " long and ripped 9 " wide
	2 adjustable shelves, 41¾ " long and ripped 8¾ " wide
	19 ' clear pine 1 x 3, cut into:
	4 stretchers, 42 " long
	1 bottom facing, 43½ " long
	15 ' clear pine 1 x 2, cut into:
	1 top facing, 43½ " long
	2 side facings, cut to fit (about 32 ")
	3 bottom trim pieces, about 70 " in all
Parting bead	64 " strip ½ " x ¾ " parting bead, cut to fit into 2 backstops
Molding	70 " strip ogee cap molding, cut to fit into 3 pieces
	70 " strip bed molding, cut to fit into 3 pieces
Plywood	1 piece ¼ " plywood, 41¾ " x 33¼ ", for back panel
Hardware	sixpenny and fourpenny nails
	1 " brads
	8 metal bracket pins
Finish	oil-based enamel
For the jig	1 clear pine 1 x 3, 31 " long

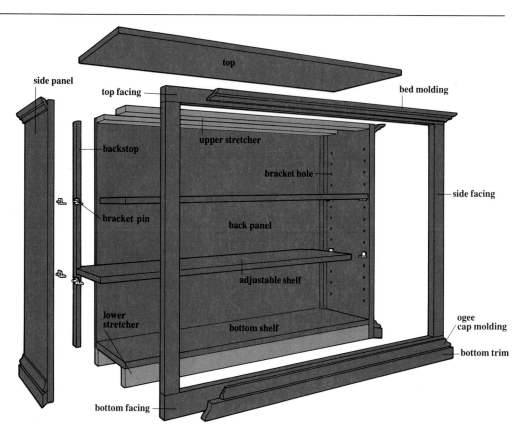

A bookcase of standard lumber. Four 1-by-3s used as stretchers, or crosspieces, are nailed to the corners of two 1-by-10 side panels to form the bookcase frame. A 1-by-12 top, 1-by-10 bottom shelf and ¼-inch plywood back panel complete the basic structure. The 1-by-2 facing around the shelf opening and the decorative molding applied to the top and bottom of the piece give it a classic look. Two adjustable shelves rest on metal bracket pins inserted into holes drilled in the side panels; any metal or plastic shelf bracket with a round shank could replace the bracket pins.

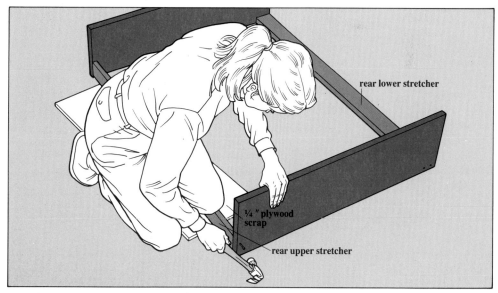

Constructing the bookcase frame. Spread carpenter's glue on one end of what will be the rear lower stretcher. Hold a side panel against it, the corners aligned. Kneeling on the stretcher to steady it, nail through the side panel into the stretcher's end with two sixpenny nails, 1 inch apart. Glue and nail the opposite end of the stretcher to the other side panel. Apply glue to both ends of the rear upper stretcher and lay it on edge between the side panels, supported by a piece of ¼-inch plywood to recess it from the side-panel edges. Align the stretcher with the ends of the side panels and nail both ends as you did with the lower stretcher. Carefully turn the assembly over and attach the front upper and lower stretchers the same way, but do not recess the upper stretcher. ▶

2 **Squaring the frame.** Before the glue in the joints sets (about 10 minutes), measure the frame from corner to corner diagonally, in both directions. If the two measurements do not match, gently press toward each other the two corners that are farther apart, then measure again. When the measurements match, brace the frame in position by nailing a length of scrap wood diagonally from the upper stretcher to the side panel at the back of the frame. Leave the brace in place for at least two hours, until the glue has dried completely.

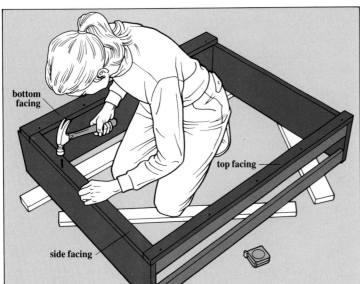

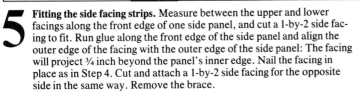

5 **Fitting the side facing strips.** Measure between the upper and lower facings along the front edge of one side panel, and cut a 1-by-2 side facing to fit. Run glue along the front edge of the side panel and align the outer edge of the facing with the outer edge of the side panel: The facing will project ¾ inch beyond the panel's inner edge. Nail the facing in place as in Step 4. Cut and attach a 1-by-2 side facing for the opposite side in the same way. Remove the brace.

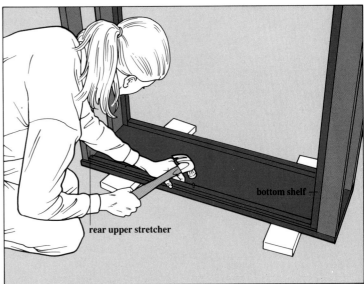

6 **Attaching the backstops.** Set the bookcase on its side on pads of scrap wood. Measure between the bottom shelf and the rear upper stretcher, along the inside, and cut a strip of parting bead to that length. Apply a line of glue to one wide side of the strip and place the glued surface on the side panel, aligning the ends of the strip with the back edge of the bottom shelf and the back edge of the rear upper stretcher. Nail the strip in place with 1-inch brads centered along it at 6-inch intervals. Turn the bookcase on its other side; measure, cut and install the second backstop.

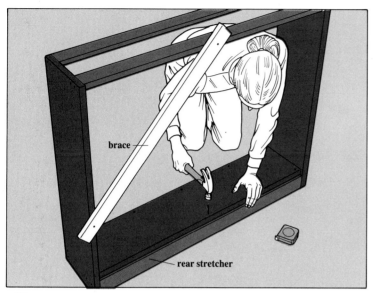

3 **Installing the bottom shelf.** Set the frame upright. Spread a line of glue along the top edges of the lower stretchers and set the bottom shelf upon them, aligning its front edge with the front stretcher: The rear edge of the shelf will cover all but ¼ inch of the rear stretcher. Drive sixpenny nails through the bottom shelf into the front stretcher, ½ inch from the edge and spaced approximately 3 inches from each end and at 10-inch intervals in between. Along the back edge of the bottom shelf, nail ¼ inch from the edge (above), nailing carefully so that the nails neither split the shelf nor miss the stretcher.

4 **Attaching the top and bottom facing strips.** Rest the frame on its back on scrap-wood pads and spread glue along the front edge of the bottom shelf and on the lower stretcher. Set the 1-by-3 bottom facing across the shelf edge and stretcher, aligning the top edge of the facing with the top of the shelf. Nail the facing to the shelf edge with fourpenny nails ½ inch from the top edge, spaced about 3 inches from the ends and every 10 inches in between (above). Apply glue along the front edge of the upper stretcher, align the 1-by-2 upper facing with the top edge of the stretcher, and nail it as you did the lower facing.

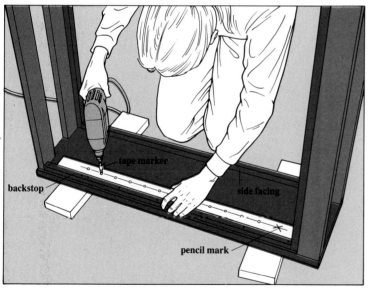

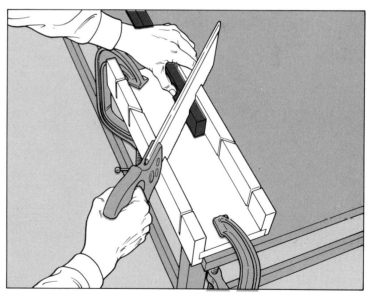

7 **Drilling bracket-pin holes.** Make a jig, or drill guide, by first drawing a line down the center of a 31-inch 1-by-3 and making tick marks at 2-inch intervals. Fit a power drill with a twist bit of the same diameter as the bracket-pin shanks, and drill a hole through the jig at each mark. Then wrap a piece of masking tape around the bit 1⅛ inch from the tip as a depth guide. Mark one end of the jig with a pencil; always place this end against the bottom shelf as you drill. Brace the jig against the backstop and the bottom shelf, and drill straight down through each hole into the side panel until the tape meets the jig. Then align the jig with the side facing and the bottom shelf, and drill a second row of holes. Turn the bookcase on its other side and repeat.

8 **Cutting trim in a miter box.** Clamp a miter box to the worktable with a pair of C clamps. Hold a 1-by-2, at least 50 inches long, narrow side up against the back wall of the miter box. Adjust the position of the 1-by-2 until its end is about 2 inches from the 45° slot in the miter box. Insert a backsaw in the slots and cut the end off the 1-by-2 (above). ▶

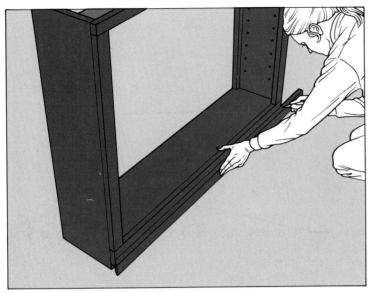

9 **Fitting the mitered trim.** Set the bookcase upright and — resting the trim on the floor — hold the trim against the bottom facing with the inner corner of the mitered end toward the bookcase. Carefully align the inner corner with the corresponding corner of the facing. At the opposite end, mark the top edge of the trim where it meets the other corner of the facing. Put the trim strip in the miter box, the mark up and against the back of the miter box. Cut the trim at the mark, at a 45° angle opposite to the first angle. Spread glue on the back of the trim, and align it against the bottom facing and along the floor. Nail the trim to the facing with fourpenny nails, centered along the trim, about 4 inches from each end and at 10-inch intervals in between.

10 **Attaching the side trim.** Cut one end of a 1-by-2, at least 14 inches long, at a 45° angle as in Step 8. Hold the trim against a side panel, fitting the angled end against the corresponding angle of the front trim. Mark the side trim where it meets the back corner of the bookcase. Align the mark with the 90° slot of the miter box, and cut the end straight. Spread glue on the back and fasten the trim in place with three fourpenny nails. Cut a similar trim piece for the opposite side and fasten it in place.

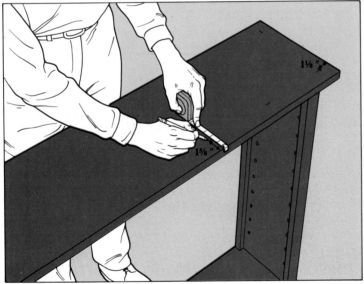

12 **Attaching the top.** Spread a thin coat of glue on the tops of the upper stretchers, side panels and facing. Position the top so that its back edge is flush with the side panels' back edges: The top will extend ¼ inch beyond the rear upper stretcher. Measure the overhang of the top at each side and slide the top, if necessary, to center it. Mark nail positions on the top, 1⅝ inches from the front and back edges and 1⅛ inches from the side edges, at 10-inch intervals. Drive a sixpenny nail at each mark.

13 **Applying bed molding under the top.** Rest the bookcase upside down, the top protected by scrap wood. Measure and cut bed molding for the front and sides as you did the 1-by-2 trim in Steps 8, 9 and 10. Use a nail set to drive the heads of the brads slightly below the surface of the molding (inset).

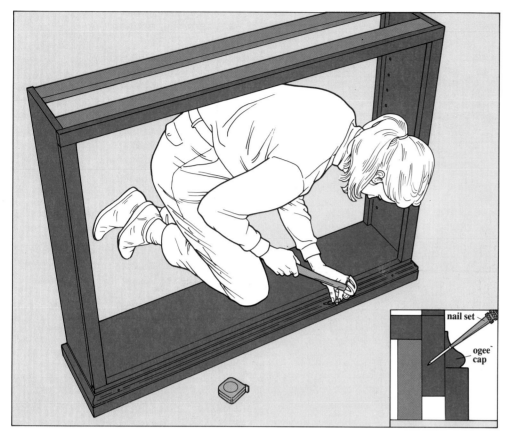

11 **Applying the ogee cap molding.** Measure and cut molding to fit the front of the bookcase, along the top of the trim, using the techniques in Steps 8 and 9. Apply glue to the back of the molding and set it in place, aligning the corners with the outside edges of the side panels.

Drive 1-inch brads into the middle of the molding at a slight downward angle, about 4 inches from each end and at 10-inch intervals in between. Drive the brads as deep as possible without letting the hammer strike the wood; finish by holding the tip of a nail set on the head of one brad at a time and tapping the butt of the nail set lightly with the hammer to recess the head *(inset)*.

Cut and glue the two side molding pieces as you did the trim in Step 10; nail each to a side panel with three 1-inch brads, using the nail set as before.

nail set

ogee cap

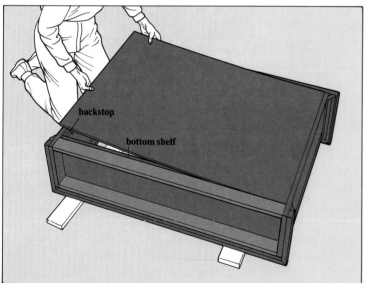

backstop

bottom shelf

14 **Inserting the back panel.** Lay the bookcase face down on scrap wood. Spread glue in the recess formed by the rear upper stretcher, the two backstops and the bottom shelf. Drop the ¼-inch plywood back panel into the recess and carefully nail it in place at 10-inch intervals with 1-inch brads, ⅛ inch from the edges.

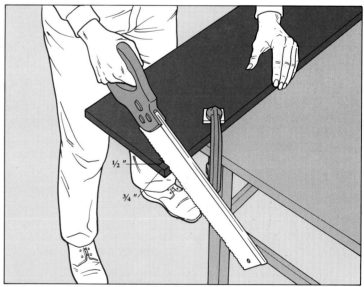

½ "

¾ "

15 **Cutting notches in the shelves.** To fit the adjustable shelves against the backstops, mark a ¾-by-½-inch rectangle at each back corner on both shelves. Clamp a shelf to the worktable with the end overhanging the table edge, the C clamp padded with a bit of scrap wood. Use the backsaw to cut off the corner at the marks. Repeat for the three other corners. Insert bracket pins into the predrilled holes in the bookcase sides, and set the shelves in place.

Clear glass on a dainty frame

Just a few slim pieces of sculpted pine molding, solidly fastened to the walls of an alcove, can support a decorative shelf of ⅜-inch glass. Since the glass weighs about 4 pounds a square foot, the alcove should not be more than about 4 feet wide by 2 feet deep; the one shown below measures 3 feet wide by 1½ feet deep.

Except for size, options abound. This shelf is recessed inside the alcove but might have been brought flush with the front walls. The molding here stops about an inch from the front of the glass — a trick that gives it the look of floating free.

The shelf can be either ordinary clear glass or — for more strength and safety — costlier tempered glass. A clear plastic, such as Plexiglas® acrylic, ½ inch thick could take the place of glass: It would be less likely to break but more likely to scratch. When buying the glass or plastic, ask the dealer to bevel or polish smooth the sharp front edges.

When measuring for the glass or plastic shelf, take the dimensions of the opening at both the back and the front. Use the smaller measurement, less ⅛ inch to be sure the shelf fits easily.

The molding shown is roman ogee cap. But a good lumber store will carry dozens of patterns, and your only limit is that the top of the molding must project in a ½- to ¾-inch flat surface to support the shelf. To determine how much molding you need, add the widths of the three walls.

Molding generally is sold in standard lengths of 8, 10, 12, 14 and 16 feet; get enough to have an extra foot or two for practice cuts. If you plan to paint the wood, buy so-called finger-jointed molding. It is made of segments that have been glued together, but it is inexpensive and as strong as the clear molding — cut from a single length of wood — that you need to buy for staining.

Finish the molding before installing it. If painting the molding, as shown here, sand it with medium (100-grit), then fine (150-grit) paper, and apply a sealer, such as shellac. Then sand with very fine (220-grit) paper and apply one or two coats of oil-based enamel. If staining the molding, apply an oil-based stain with cheese-cloth, wipe with a dry cloth, then apply a mineral-spirit sealer. When it dries, sand with medium (100-grit) sandpaper, then apply clear varnish.

To achieve the most attractive appearance, the molding has to be fitted together where strips meet at the back corners. The simplest way to do this is to use a backsaw and miter box to cut 45° angles at the ends of the molding strips. Unless the walls meet at perfect right angles, however, you will need gobs of spackling compound to fill gaps between the pieces.

A surer way to produce snug corners is demonstrated here: The ends of the back molding are cut straight, and the rear ends of the sidepieces are mitered and coped — cut with a coping saw — into mirror images of the profile of the backpiece.

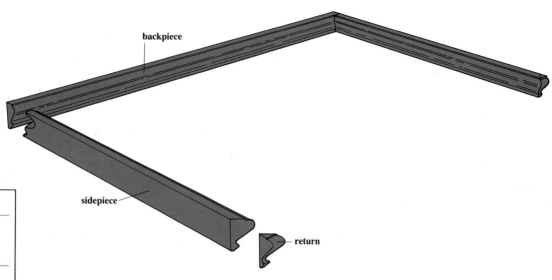

backpiece

sidepiece

return

Materials List

Molding	8 ′ roman ogee cap pine molding, cut into: 1 piece, 48 ″ long 2 pieces, 24 ″ long
Nails	8 sixpenny finishing nails
Glass	⅜ ″-thick glass, cut ⅛ ″ smaller in each dimension than the space it is to fit
Finish	oil-based enamel

Three-sided support. When the wood molding supporting the back and sides of a shelf is on display, the effect is most attractive if the sidepieces are contoured, or coped, to interlock over the backpiece. At each forward end of the support, a small mitered piece called a return continues the curved face of the molding around from the side to the front.

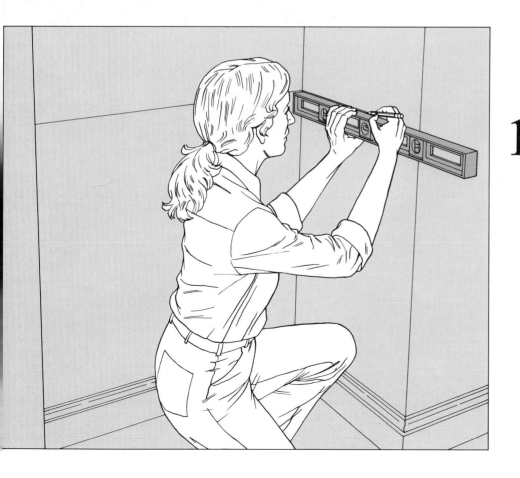

1 **Drawing level shelf lines.** Finish the strips of molding with enamel. Then, holding the end of a tape measure at the floor in the center of the alcove's rear wall, measure up 36 inches and pencil a mark on the wall. With a 2-foot level as a straightedge, pencil a line through the mark and across the wall. From each corner, continue the line onto the side walls *(left)*. Locate the studs *(page 21),* if any, and mark each one by making a tick across the shelf line.

Measure across the back shelf line, then mark this distance on the contoured side of the 48-inch molding strip. Clamp a miter box to your worktable *(page 31, Step 8).* Place the molding in the box, flat side down, push it against the back of the box and align the pencil mark with the 90° slot. Hold the molding firmly and use a backsaw to cut it at the mark. ▶

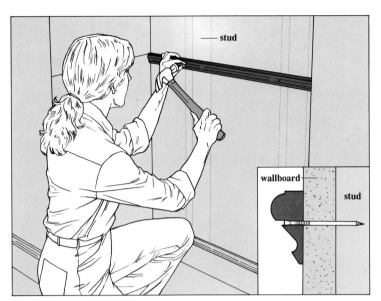

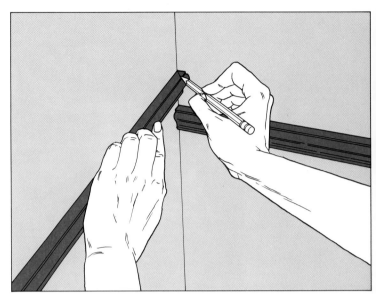

2 **Fitting the rear molding.** Place the molding against the rear wall with its flat top just below the shelf line. Hammer a sixpenny finishing nail through the molding at each stud, nailing straight into the wall below the broad top curve *(inset)*. Lacking studs, use 2-inch-long No. 10 wood screws with anchors for a masonry wall or ³⁄₁₆-inch toggle bolts 3 inches long for a hollow wall *(Appendix, page 125);* insert two in evenly spaced, counterbored holes. Leave the ends of the molding free; they will be secured by coped side molding later.

Use a nail set *(page 33, Step 11)* to countersink the nails. Squeeze wood plastic into each nail hole; smooth the surface with a finger. Let the wood plastic dry and shrink; then repeat the application.

3 **Mitering the left side molding.** Place a 24-inch piece of molding against the left-hand wall. Hold the molding's far end above the rear-wall molding. Sketch an approximate 45° angle along the flat top and first curve of the side-wall molding *(above)*. Next, use a C clamp and a protective wood scrap to hold the marked end of the side-wall molding in the miter box with the molding's flat side against the far wall of the box and its broad curve uppermost. Use a backsaw to cut a 45° angle through the molding along the sketched line.

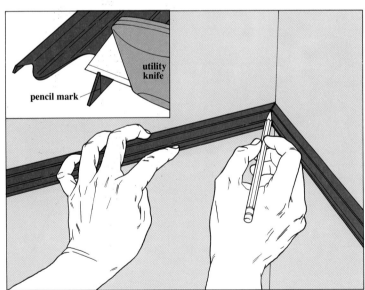

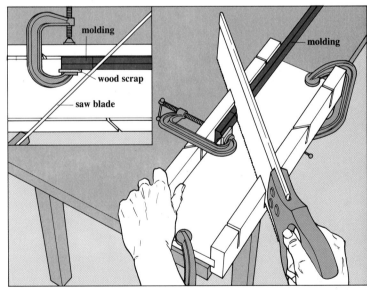

5 **Making a smooth support surface.** Fit the coped end of your left-hand wall molding onto the rear-wall molding. The top of the coped molding will stand a little above the rear molding. To create a flat surface for your shelf, make a pencil mark on the top of the coped molding *(above)* at the first ridge in the top curve of the rear-wall molding. At the worktable, use a ruler to draw a straight line from the mark to the back of the molding. Gently score the line three or four times with a utility knife; then slice along the line firmly *(inset)*.

6 **Mitering the side support.** Just above the left-hand wall's shelf line, pencil a mark 2 inches from the front end of the wall. Position the coped molding on the wall and mark it at the same point. At the worktable, use a ruler to draw a straight line across the top of the molding from the mark. Draw a 45° angle on the molding from the front end of the pencil line toward the right. Set the marked end of the molding in the miter box at the same 45° slot used for the first cut *(Step 3);* lay the flat back of the molding against the far wall of the miter box and align the angled line with the diagonal slot. Using scrap wood to protect the molding, clamp it snugly *(inset)*. Cut a 45° angle through the molding.

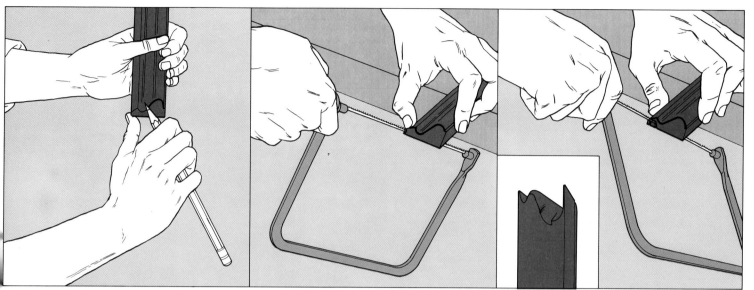

4 **Coping the left side molding.** Color in the profile of the molding at the end just cut, using the side of a pencil lead to rub along the ridge *(above, left)*. Place the molding, flat side down, on the worktable and extend the angled end beyond the table's edge. If you are right-handed, use your left hand to hold the wood on the table and your right hand to manage the coping saw; if you are left-handed, reverse these positions.

Start cutting along the narrow edge first *(above, center)*. Tilt the saw back toward the underside of the table; use a finger to help support the weak end at the first cut; then start with gentle pushing motions of the saw, cutting along the bottom edge of your colored line. Do not turn the blade. When you reach the crest of the small first curve,

make a relief cut by removing the saw and — from a point farther right — cutting back to where you had to stop *(above, right)*.

After making the first two delicate cuts, move to the broad curve at the right and cut from right to left, using both pushing and pulling strokes from now on. Keep the blade tilted back toward the table. Make straight cuts along the penciled line and a relief cut whenever you need to turn the saw blade, until the piece is fully coped, as seen in the inset where it is inverted to show its underside.

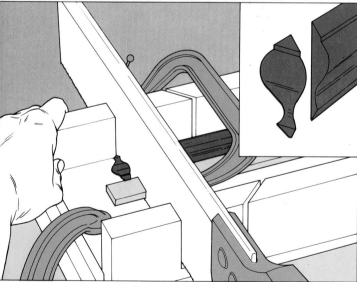

7 **Making a return.** Use the backsaw and miter box to cut a piece of scrap molding at the opposite 45° angle from the last cut. Then lay the molding, flat side down, in the miter box with its narrower curve against the back *(above)*, and put lath against it for strength: The triangle to be cut is fragile at the narrow point. Place the bottom edge of the mitered molding just to the left of the 90° slot. Cut through lath as well as molding. Before gluing, check the fit of the left-hand wall molding against the return *(inset)*. Squeeze contact cement onto the faces to be joined, wait five to 15 minutes until the cemented surfaces are tacky and glossy, then put the pieces together.

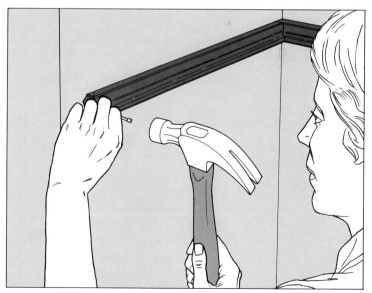

8 **Finishing the shelf supports.** Repeat Steps 3 through 7 to make the right-hand wall molding; be sure to reverse the direction of the 45° angles. Let the cemented return corners dry overnight, then use very fine (220-grit) sandpaper to smooth the molding joints. Nail the side-wall moldings to studs with fourpenny nails or, if there are no studs, counterbore holes for the appropriate alternate fasteners *(Step 2)*. Countersink the nails and fill the holes with vinyl spackling compound.

When the shelf supports are in place, check for gaps between wall and molding. Fill any spaces with spackle; let it dry. Then touch up the finish of the molding, if necessary, and set the glass shelf on top of it.

An inside track to sleek style

Form follows function smoothly in the spare interpretation of the indispensable wall system shown below. The effortless intersection of horizontal shelves and vertical columns masks the intrinsic sturdiness of the unit. Finished in your choice of enamel, varnish or penetrating oil, this system is at home with styles as diverse as Scandinavian modern, Art Deco and Italian avant-garde.

The floating effect of the shelves is achieved by hiding bracket tracks, or standards *(pages 22-23)*, in slots in the backs of wood columns lined up a foot or so from a wall. The brackets and the shelves they hold thus extend toward the rear, leaving the wall clear of hardware.

To form slots for the standards, each column comprises two 1-by-3s laminated to the sides of a 1-by-2. Horizontal arms, camouflaged by permanently fixed top and bottom shelves, connect the columns with the wall.

The columns here are spaced 3 feet apart, center to center; the shelves extend 8 feet. The columns can be closer together — or as much as 42 inches apart — and the number of columns can be adjusted to fit any wall width. The top and bottom shelves must always span the complete range; other shelves could be shorter and placed at staggered levels.

Constructing the shelf system is easy. You can have all the boards cut at the lumberyard, or just ask to have the 1-by-12 shelves sawed to order, and cut the 1-by-2s and 1-by-3s yourself — using a miter box to guide a handsaw for uniform square ends. With all of the components cut to length, you then need only fit them

together with glue and nails as demonstrated on the following pages. Careful measuring and a combination square will ensure perfect 90° joints.

If your wall has baseboard molding, measure its thickness and subtract that amount from the length of each lower support-arm piece. In addition, if the baseboard has a shoe molding, you will need to cut notches (Step 8) in the assembled support arms to fit around it.

Before you install the bookshelf, sand the columns and the shelves first with medium (100-grit), then with fine (150-grit) sandpaper, and apply several coats of penetrating wood oil, sanding between coats with very fine (220-grit) sandpaper.

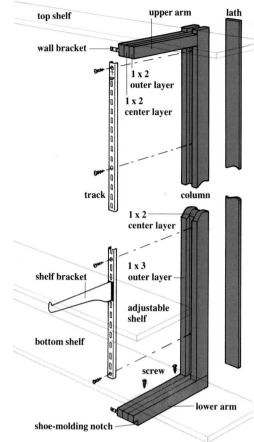

Materials List

1 x 12	40 ′ clear pine 1 x 12, cut into 5 shelves, 8′ long
1 x 3	39 ′ clear pine 1 x 3, cut into 6 column outer layers, 78 ″ long
1 x 2	39 ′ clear pine 1 x 2, cut into: 3 column center layers, 74 ″ long; 3 upper-arm center layers, 15 ″ long; 6 upper-arm outer layers, 12½ ″ long; 3 lower-arm center layers, 15 ″ long, minus thickness of baseboard; 6 lower-arm outer layers, 12½ ″ long, minus thickness of baseboard
Lath	20 ′ clear pine lath, ¼ ″ x 1¾ ″, cut into 3 strips, 78 ″ long
Bracket hardware	3 lengths metal bracket track, 6 ′ long, with screws; 15 metal shelf brackets, 12 ″ long
Fasteners	16-gauge brads, 1¼ ″ long; fourpenny finishing nails; 12 No. 8 brass-plated screws, 1½ ″ long; 6 brass-plated angle irons, 2 ″ long; 24 No. 6 brass-plated screws, 1 ″ long (for fastening brackets); 6 wall anchors
Finish	penetrating wood oil

A column of shelves. Two upright 1-by-3s sandwich a 1-by-2, creating a recess that hides a shelf-bracket track. The center layers of the top and bottom arms are also sandwiched by the 1-by-3s, forming strong joints. Lath covers the front edges and ends. Two 1-by-12 shelves are permanently screwed to the arms to brace them; the track between the arms holds brackets for adjustable shelves. Angle irons fix the ends of the arms to the wall. A notch in the lower arm accommodates baseboard shoe molding.

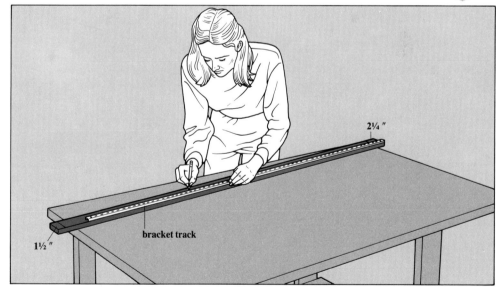

1 **Marking the outer layer of a column.** Lay a 78-inch 1-by-3 on the worktable, poorer-quality side up. Using a combination square, mark a perpendicular line across the board 2¼ inches from one end to indicate the position of the upper support arm. Mark a line 1½ inches from the opposite end to indicate the lower support-arm position. To mark the recess for the bracket track, align the track, slots upward, along what will be the back edge of the 1-by-3. Using the track as a straightedge, draw a line along the 1-by-3 between the support-arm marks (above). ▶

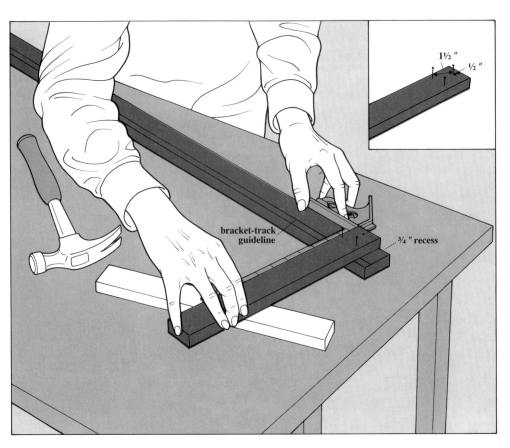

2 **Attaching support-arm center layers.** Tap three brads partway into one end of a 15-inch 1-by-2: Center one brad ½ inch from the end and set a pair of brads 1½ inches from it to form a triangle *(inset)*. Spread glue on the back of the 1-by-2, behind the brads. Align the bottom edge of the glued end with the upper support-arm position line and its end with the front edge of the 1-by-3; support the arm's free end with scrap wood. There will be a ¾-inch recess between the 1-by-2 and the end of the 1-by-3. Drive a single brad; then, with the aid of a combination square *(right)*, position the 1-by-2 at a 90° angle to the 1-by-3 and drive the remaining brads. Attach the center layer of the lower support arm the same way.

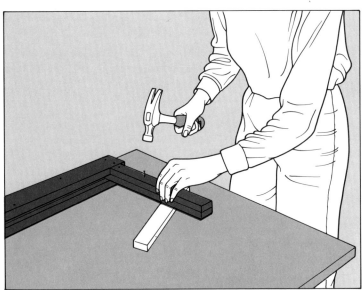

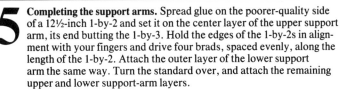

5 **Completing the support arms.** Spread glue on the poorer-quality side of a 12½-inch 1-by-2 and set it on the center layer of the upper support arm, its end butting the 1-by-3. Hold the edges of the 1-by-2s in alignment with your fingers and drive four brads, spaced evenly, along the length of the 1-by-2. Attach the outer layer of the lower support arm the same way. Turn the standard over, and attach the remaining upper and lower support-arm layers.

6 **Attaching lath.** Set the column on its back, with the support arms hanging off the worktable. Run a bead of glue along the front edge of each 1-by-3. Center a lath strip along the front of the column, its ends even with the ends of the 1-by-3s. Drive pairs of brads (one brad into each 1-by-3) at 8-inch intervals, starting 1 inch from one end. The lath may be warped; before driving each pair of brads, center the lath with your fingers. Use a nail set to recess the heads of all nails and brads in the column, and fill the holes with wood putty.

3 **Adding the column's center layer.** Run several beads of glue along the center of the 1-by-3. Align one edge of a 74-inch 1-by-2 with the lengthwise guideline on the 1-by-3. Drive brads every 6 inches, in a staggered pattern, down the length of the 1-by-2. The wood may be warped; before driving each brad, straighten the board along the guideline.

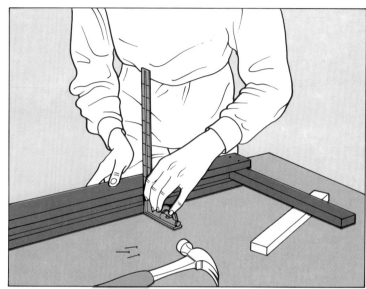

4 **Attaching the final outer layer.** Run continuous beads of glue along the 1-by-2 center layer and set a 78-inch 1-by-3 on top of it — with its better side upward. With a combination square, align the ends and sides of the two 1-by-3 outer layers. Drive two fourpenny nails at the top end of the 1-by-3 into the 1-by-2 support arm below it. Drive fourpenny nails every 8 inches down the length of the 1-by-3 into the 1-by-2 center layer, staggering the nail positions slightly. Adjust the alignment of the 1-by-3s with the square before driving each nail *(above)*. Drive two nails through the 1-by-3 into the lower support arm.

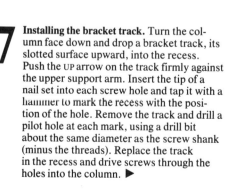

7 **Installing the bracket track.** Turn the column face down and drop a bracket track, its slotted surface upward, into the recess. Push the UP arrow on the track firmly against the upper support arm. Insert the tip of a nail set into each screw hole and tap it with a hammer to mark the recess with the position of the hole. Remove the track and drill a pilot hole at each mark, using a drill bit about the same diameter as the screw shank (minus the threads). Replace the track in the recess and drive screws through the holes into the column. ▶

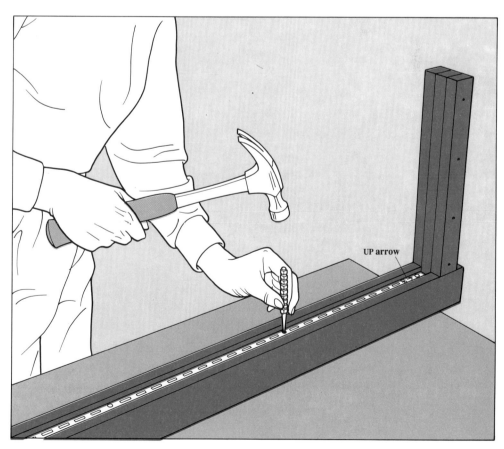

UP arrow

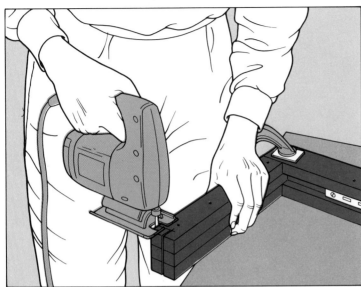

8 Notching the lower support arm. Measure the height of your baseboard shoe molding — if any — and the distance it protrudes from the wall. Use a combination square and pencil to outline a rectangle of these dimensions at the bottom corner of the lower support arm. Lay the column on the worktable with the end of the support arm hanging over the edge. Clamp the column in place. Fit a saber saw with a blade made for cutting a thickness of 2¼ inches. Then saw a notch in the arm by cutting along one line at a time from the edge of the support arm to the point where the lines intersect. The first shelf standard is now complete. Follow Steps 1 through 8 to make two more standards identical to the first, then finish the standards and shelves.

9 Installing the first column. Screw one leg of a 2-inch brass-plated angle iron lengthwise on the right side of the end of each support arm. Mark a vertical line on the baseboard where you want to position the left-hand side of the leftmost column. Hold the column upright at the mark; brace the lower arm against the baseboard with your toe. Holding a level against the side of the column, move the column left or right until it is vertical, then mark the positions of the angle-iron holes on the wall and baseboard. Set the column aside. Drill pilot holes at the marks, and insert screw anchors in the holes in the wall. Reposition the standard and drive 1-inch No. 6 brass-plated screws through the angle irons into the wall and baseboard.

If the upper angle iron aligns with a wall stud, do not insert screw anchors; instead, fasten the angle iron with 1½-inch No. 6 wood screws.

column-position line

baseboard

shoe molding

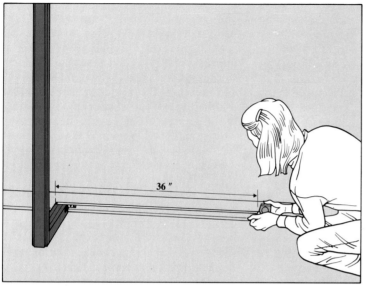

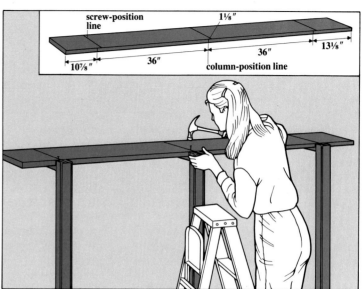

10 **Installing successive standards.** Hook the end of a steel measuring tape over the lower support arm of the first column, measure 36 inches to the right, and mark a vertical line on the baseboard for the position of the second column. Measure and mark the wall 36 inches to the right of the upper support arm. Align the left-hand sides of the support arms of the second column with the marks, checking its verticality with a level. Mark angle-iron screw positions, drill pilot holes and install the column as in Step 9. Install the remaining column the same way.

11 **Positioning the top shelf.** To mark a 1-by-12 shelf for alignment with the columns *(inset)*, first use a combination square and pencil to draw a vertical mark on the front edge 10⅞ inches from the left-hand end. Then make two more marks along the edge at 36-inch intervals; the last mark will be 13⅛ inches from the right end. To indicate screw positions, draw lines across the face of the shelf 1⅛ inches to the right of each mark. Rest the shelf on the upper support arms, its front edge flush against the backs of the columns. Carefully align each column with the corresponding front-edge mark, and tack the shelf in place by driving one fourpenny nail partway into each support arm *(above)*.

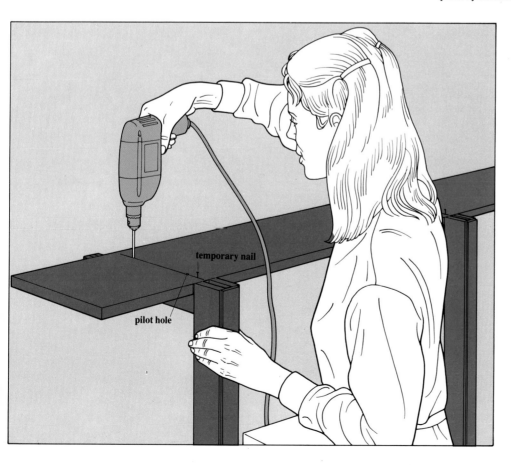

12 **Fastening the top shelf.** At each of the three column-position guidelines, drill two pilot holes through the shelf into the support arm — one hole 3 inches from the front edge and the other 3 inches from the back edge. Drive 1½-inch No. 8 brass-plated screws through the holes, then pull out the temporary nails. Install the bottom shelf as you did the top shelf. Hook shelf brackets onto the bracket tracks where desired, and set the adjustable shelves in place.

Ladder shelves: Spare but strong

The delicate look of ladder-supported shelf units belies their strength. Whether anchored to a wall singly or in rows or hinged to form a freestanding room divider, these versatile units can bear even such weighty loads as records and books.

The frame of each ladder is made from ¾-inch pine molding stock. Brackets snap into place between ladder rungs, and shelves are screwed onto the brackets. Each of the ladder's two legs comprises three layers: The rung ends and the spacers that separate them are sandwiched between two long molding strips.

The ladder may be of any width up to 24 inches; fully laden shelves wider than that would put too much stress on the rungs. The height is limited only by the available length of molding strips: For most floor-to-ceiling units, 8-foot lengths suffice. To allow for clearance when the units are mounted, the legs are ¼ inch shorter than the distance from floor to ceiling.

The ladders pictured here are of ceiling height and either 18½ or 24 inches wide. The 18½-inch versions flanking the chair below are secured to studs with wood screws and angle irons. The angle irons, attached inside the legs, are 16 inches apart — the common spacing for studs. The legs on ladders of other widths, or on a row of ladders installed side by side, are likely to meet the wall between studs and must be anchored with hollow-wall or masonry fasteners (page 125).

Constructing a unit with level rungs and straight legs requires a jig — an open-ended rectangle of lath strips nailed to particleboard — to guide the placement of the molding strips. On the jig shown on page 47, the lath sidepieces sit 18½ inches apart to yield a ladder that wide. By repositioning one sidepiece, the same jig can be used to build units of other widths.

Once the ladder has been assembled, a lath strip may be nailed along the outsides of the legs to disguise the details of their construction. Or the sides may be left unadorned to present stripes of contrasting wood grains. If you plan to fasten units side by side (box, page 50), separate them with a single lath strip; for ladders that are to be hinged together (box, page 51), add the lath to all the units.

The brackets and shelves are put together after the ladder has been installed. The brackets are cut from 1-by-6 pine boards, actually 5½ inches wide, matching the rung spacing; notches at the back of each bracket accommodate the rungs. The shelves may be cut from boards ranging in size from 1-by-6 to 1-by-12.

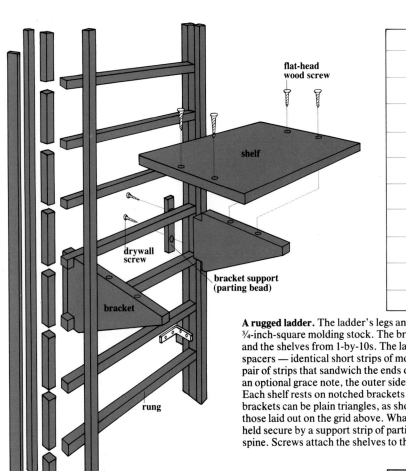

flat-head
wood screw

shelf

drywall
screw

bracket support
(parting bead)

bracket

rung

molding strip

spacer

decorative lath strip

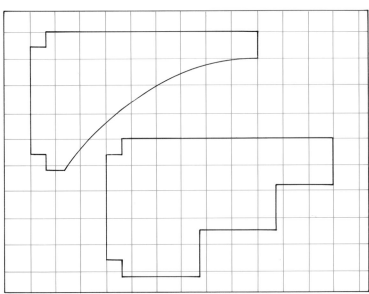

A rugged ladder. The ladder's legs and rungs are made entirely of ¾-inch-square molding stock. The brackets are cut from 1-by-6 boards and the shelves from 1-by-10s. The ladder's rungs are separated by spacers — identical short strips of molding stock. Each leg consists of a pair of strips that sandwich the ends of the rungs and their spacers. As an optional grace note, the outer sides of the legs are covered with lath. Each shelf rests on notched brackets wedged between the rungs. The brackets can be plain triangles, as shown at left, or contoured forms like those laid out on the grid above. Whatever its shape, each bracket is held secure by a support strip of parting-bead molding screwed to its spine. Screws attach the shelves to the brackets.

Materials List (for one ladder unit)

Wood	10 strips ¾ " x ¾ " molding stock, 8 ' long 1 piece ¾ " x ½ " parting bead, 5 ' long 2 strips ¼ " x 1¾ " lath, 8 ' long 8 ' clear pine 1 x 6 8 ' clear pine 1 x 10
Fasteners	16-gauge finishing brads, 1¼ " long ¼ lb. fourpenny finishing nails 24 No. 8 flat-head brass-plated or zinc-chromate-plated wood screws, 1½ " long 32 No. 8 drywall screws, 1¼ " long 16 No. 6 wood screws, 8 of them ⅝ " long, 8 of them 1½ " long 4 brass-plated or galvanized-steel angle irons, with 1½ " legs
Finish	oil-based sealer oil-based enamel with a satin or mat finish

For the jig	1 piece ⅝ " particleboard, 30 " x 8 '
	19 ' lath, ¼ " x 1¾ ", cut into:
	    2 strips, 8 ' long
	    1 strip, 30 " long
	2 strips ¼ " x 1¾ " lath, 8 ' long
	24 16-gauge finishing brads, ¾ " long

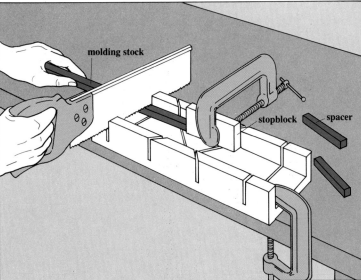

molding stock

stopblock   spacer

3 **Cutting the spacers.** Clamp a piece of scrap wood inside a miter box, positioning its end 4 inches from the near edge of one 90° slot so that the scrap will serve as a stopblock. Slide an 8-foot piece of molding stock into the miter box, butting its end against the stopblock, and saw off a section with a backsaw (*above*). Measure the cut piece to ensure that it is 4 inches long; if necessary, adjust the stopblock. Then continue cutting spacers, keeping the area between the slot and the stopblock free of sawdust to avoid skewing the measurement. Measure the cut spacers; discard any that are not identical.

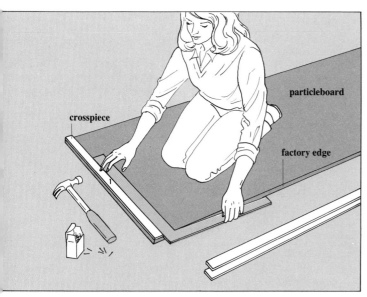

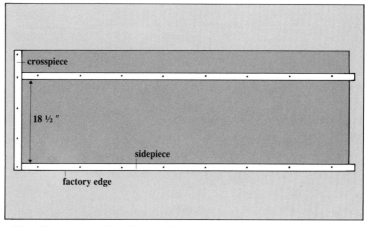

1 **Attaching the jig crosspiece.** Align one long edge of the 30-inch lath strip with one end of the particleboard. Tack the lath at its midpoint to the board with a ¾-inch-long brad, letting the head of the brad protrude about ¼ inch above the surface. Holding a carpenter's square so that one leg lines up against the inside edge of the lath and the other leg slopes downward along the factory-finished side edge of the particleboard, check the angle between the lath and the board; adjust the lath, if necessary, to square it. Tack the lath in place with four or five more brads.

2 **Completing the jig.** Align one long edge of an 8-foot lath strip with the long factory edge of the particleboard, butting the top end of the strip against the inside edge of the crosspiece. Use a carpenter's square to ensure that the two pieces are perpendicular. Then tack the sidepiece to the board with ¾-inch brads spaced 12 inches apart, leaving the brad heads ¼ inch above the surface. Measure and make a tick mark 18½ inches from the inside edge of the sidepiece at the top, middle and bottom. Position a second 8-foot lath with its inside edge touching the tick marks; tack it in place as you did the first strip. Remeasure the distance between the two sidepieces at the tick marks; if necessary, pry one piece loose and adjust its position. Hammer the brads down.

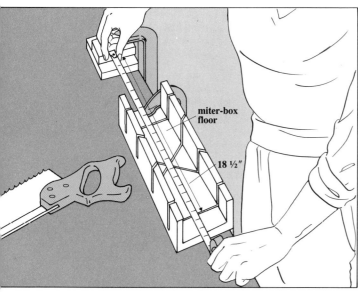

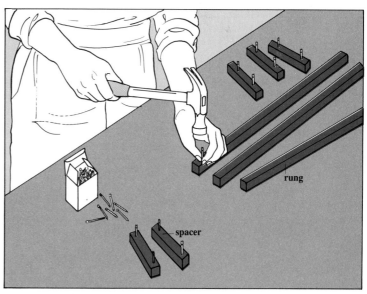

4 **Cutting the rungs.** Move the stopblock to a position 18½ inches from the 90° slot, and clamp it to the work surface, resting it on a larger wood scrap of the same thickness as the miter-box floor. Check the measurement between the stopblock and the slot *(above),* then slide a strip of molding stock into the box, resting its end on the wood scrap and butting it against the stopblock. Cut off a section and check to see that it fits exactly between the parallel sidepieces on the jig; if it does not, adjust the position of the stopblock. Cut as many rungs as you need, keeping the stopblock and miter box free of accumulated sawdust.

5 **Starting the nails.** After you have cut all of the spacers and rungs, hammer two brads ¼ inch deep into each piece: For spacers, place the brads 1 inch from each end; for rungs, place them ⅜ inch from each end. TIP: Beforehand, blunt the point of each brad by tapping it with the hammer; this reduces the risk of splitting the wood. Also, examine each piece for defects. For the rungs, drive the brads into the most perfect looking surfaces; thus, sides slightly gouged or splintered during cutting will face up or down on the upright ladder and be less conspicuous. For the spacers, start the nails in the imperfect sides; they will then be concealed by the long molding strips. ▶

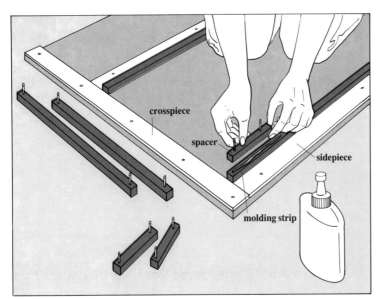

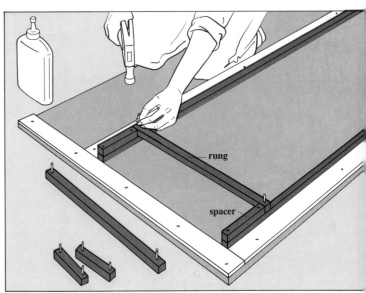

6 **Attaching the spacers.** Cut four 8-foot pieces of molding stock into strips the desired height of the ladder. Lay two strips on the jig, one inside each sidepiece; butt the end of each strip tightly against the crosspiece. Starting from the top, squeeze a thin line of wood glue 5 inches long down the face of one of the strips. Lay a spacer on top of the glue, aligning its sides and top end with those of the molding strip. Holding the spacer steady with one hand, hammer in the preset brads. Use a damp cloth to wipe away any glue that seeps out. Attach a spacer to the opposite strip in the same fashion.

7 **Attaching the rungs.** Lay a rung across the strips directly below the first pair of spacers, setting its ends on the glue lines. Butt the rung tightly against the spacers and align its ends with the outside edges of the two molding strips. Hammer in the preset brads (*above*). Continue gluing and nailing spacers and rungs, butting all the pieces tightly together as you work your way down the jig. End with a pair of spacers — the last rung should be no closer than 3 inches to the bottom of the ladder. Attach the two last spacers even if they jut past the ends of the molding strips.

10 **Mounting the ladder.** To accommodate any baseboard, cut four ¾-inch-wide, 3-inch-long mounting blocks the thickness of the baseboard. Paint the blocks to match the wall and let them dry. Then align each block's edges with the ladder's back edges at the top and center of each leg. Pencil in marks to show the positions of the blocks; then attach the blocks, using wood glue and two drywall screws per block.

Using ⅝-inch No. 6 screws, attach a 1½-inch angle iron to the inside of each mounting block and its leg, placing the free leg of the angle iron flush with the rear face of the block.

Locate a pair of studs (*page 21*) on which to mount the ladder. Then hold the ladder against the wall, with the free angle-iron legs aligned with the studs, and check for plumb with a level. Mark through the screw holes in all of the angle irons (*right*) and set the ladder aside. Drill pilot holes through the marks on the stud locations; lacking studs, implant hollow-wall fasteners (*page 125*). Reposition the ladder and use 1½-inch No. 6 screws to anchor it to the wall.

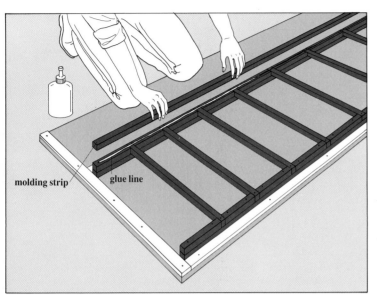

molding strip

glue line

8 **Attaching the second pair of molding strips.** Apply wood glue down the center of the spacers and across the rung ends on one side of the ladder. Lay an 8-foot molding strip on top of the glue line *(above)*, aligning its sides with those of the spacers. Nail the strip down, driving fourpenny finishing nails through every second spacer. Attach the other molding strip the same way. Let the glue dry overnight. Trim the bottom spacers even with the ends of the molding strips and sand the bottom of both legs. Set the exposed nails with a nail set *(page 33, Step 11)* and fill the recesses with wood putty applied from a tube. Slightly overfill each indentation to allow for shrinkage. Let the putty dry overnight, then use medium (100-grit) sandpaper to smooth all surfaces.

1¾ " lath

9 **Finishing the ladder.** Cut the two 8-foot strips of lath to the exact height of the ladder. Stand the ladder on its side and apply a thin line of wood glue down the center of the spacers and rung ends from top to bottom. Center a lath strip over the side and nail it in place with a row of brads on each side. Finally, seal the wood with shellac and finish it with one or two coats of oil-based enamel, sanding well with very fine (220-grit) paper between coats.

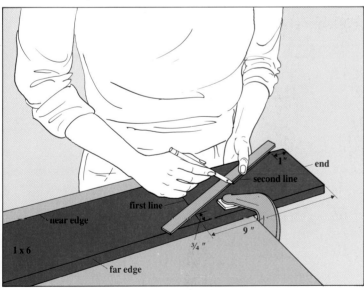

1"

end

second line

first line

near edge

9 "

¾ "

1 x 6

far edge

11 **Outlining the master bracket.** Clamp a 1-by-6 to the worktable, letting 6 inches extend over the edge. (Slipping a wood scrap between the clamp and the board will prevent marring.) Mark the edge of the board 9 inches from the end and use a carpenter's square to draw a line from that mark across the board. Mark the line ¾ inch from the far edge; make another mark on the near edge of the board, 1 inch from the end. With a straightedge, draw a second line connecting the two marks *(above)*.

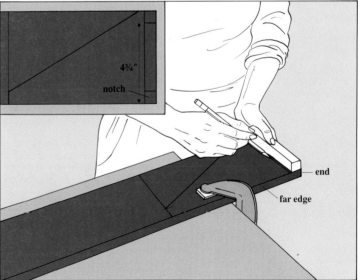

4¾"

notch

end

far edge

12 **Marking notches.** To mark notches, align the outside edge of a scrap of ¾-inch molding stock with the end of the board and trace its inside edge with a pencil *(above)*. Then align the scrap's outside edge with the far edge of the board; tracing along the scrap's inside edge, draw a short line from the end of the board to intersect the closest perpendicular. Measure between the tops of two neighboring rungs on the ladder and make a tick mark on the perpendicular at that distance — 4¾ inches in the illustration — from the far edge of the board. Use a carpenter's square to draw a second short line to the end of the board at that point. The bracket will be marked as in the inset, with two long cutting lines and a pair of notches. ▶

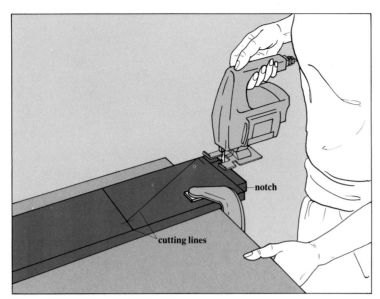

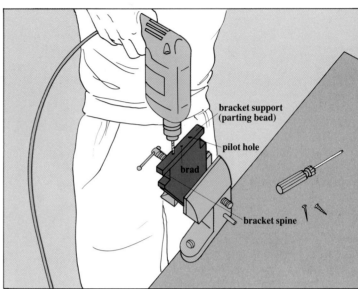

13 **Cutting the master bracket.** Reclamp the bracket to the worktable with its marked notches extending just beyond the edge. Use a saber saw to cut out the two notches *(above),* taking care not to saw past the intersection of the cutting lines. Then use a handsaw to cut the bracket along the two long cutting lines you drew in Step 11.

14 **Attaching the bracket support.** Set up a miter box and stopblock as in Step 3 to cut parting bead into bracket supports as long as the distance from the top of one rung to the bottom of the rung below it — about 5½ inches. Cut one support, then put the master bracket in a vise, and nail the support to the bracket spine with a 1¼-inch brad in the center. Attach masking tape 1¼ inches from the tip of a ³⁄₃₂-inch bit to gauge the depth of the pilot hole. Drill a 1¼-inch hole 1½ inches from each end of the support, through the support and into the bracket spine, stopping when the tape reaches the wood surface. Screw the support to the bracket with two 1¼-inch No. 8 drywall screws. Release the bracket from the vise.

Connecting Ladders

17 **Attaching the shelves.** Snap a pair of brackets in place on the ladder. Place a shelf on the brackets with its back edge flush with the back edge of the rung. Insert an awl through each of the shelf's screw holes to mark their positions on the tops of the brackets *(above).* Remove the shelves and the brackets. With a ⅛-inch drill bit, drill ¾-inch-deep pilot holes in the tops of the brackets at the marked points. Put the brackets back on the ladder. Finally, reposition the shelves and screw them to the brackets using 1½-inch-long No. 8 flat-head screws.

Connecting ladders. Attach a lath strip *(page 49, Step 9)* to only one outside edge of each ladder. Then turn a ladder on its side with the lath facing up and stack on top of it a second ladder with the lath also up. With a helper steadying the ladders, align the ends and sides of the legs. Drill a bolt hole ¼ inch in diameter through the center of the legs at the middle and 11½ inches from the top and bottom *(above).* Use the upper ladder as a guide to drill holes through the lath-strip side of any more ladders to be attached in the series. Fit pairs of ladders together with a single strip of lath between them and a washer at each end of the bolts *(inset).* Add lath to the free outside edge of the first ladder in the series.

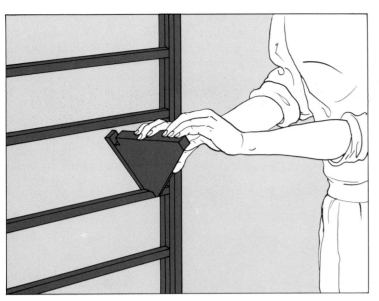

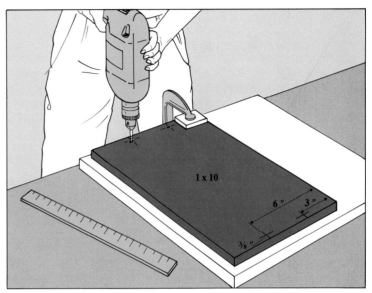

15 **Fitting the bracket.** Test the assembled master bracket for fit by wedging it between two rungs *(above)*. If necessary, remove the bracket support and trim or sand the notches in the bracket to fit the rungs. When the master bracket fits perfectly, use it as a pattern to trace and cut all of the remaining brackets you need. Cut a support for each bracket and attach it as in Step 14, putting a thin line of wood glue down the center of the bracket spine before nailing and screwing the support to it.

16 **Drilling the shelves.** Cut a 1-by-10 into shelves ⅛ inch shorter than the distance between the inside edges of the ladder legs. At each end of a shelf, ⅜ inch from the cut end, drill two counter-sunk screw holes, one 3 inches from the back of the shelf, the other 6 inches from the back. Sand and paint the brackets and the shelves to match the ladder; let them dry.

Forming a Hinged Screen

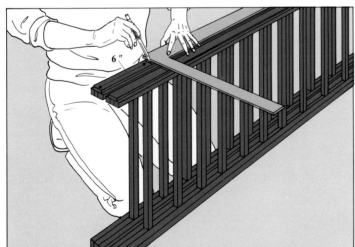

1 **Hinging the first standard.** Attach lath *(page 49, Step 9)* to the out-sides of each ladder. Place two ladders on their sides, with the ends aligned. On the outside of one leg, make marks 6 inches from each end and 1 inch above the midpoint. With a carpenter's square, draw lines across the two legs at each mark *(above)*. Set one ladder aside. On the other ladder, align the top of a 2-inch butt hinge with the top line and the hinge-pin side of the leaf with the edge of the lath. Mark the position of each screw hole on the lath. Then mark for the screw holes of hinges aligned with the middle and bottom lines. Drill a pilot hole ½ inch deep at each mark. Screw the hinges in place.

2 **Hinging the second standard.** Again align the ends of the two ladders, keeping the sides ½ inch apart. Lap the free leaf of each hinge over the lath on the second ladder. Adjust the ladders so that the hinge pins are centered between them and the free leaf of each hinge is aligned with the line on the second leg. Mark the screw-hole positions on the lath. Set the first ladder aside. Drill a ½-inch-deep pilot hole at each mark on the second ladder. Reposition the two ladders side by side, align the screw holes in the hinges with their pilot holes in the lath, and screw the free leaves to the second leg. Use the same technique to hinge as many additional ladders as you plan to include in the screen.

Freestanding frames

The rectangular frames bracing the shelves shown below are not what they seem. Far from being composed of four pieces of solid wood, the frames are paired ladders of laminated wood connected at top and bottom with laminated crossbars.

Each leg of each ladder consists of two 1-by-2s that sandwich the vertical spacers between the rungs as well as the ends of the rungs themselves. The spacers and rungs are made from ¾-inch-square molding stock; although the rung ends go all the way through the leg to its outside edge, the spacers extend only halfway. Thus each leg has a channel interrupted by rung ends along its outside edge. Filler blocks cut from the molding stock plug both ends of the channel, and lath conceals the rest. The crossbars are composed of the same elements (Step 6).

The goal of all this cabinetmaking legerdemain is to form freestanding shelf supports that are sturdy yet lightweight. Each shelf is anchored to the supports with screws driven through the rungs.

The height, depth and width of the assembly may be varied. Here, the supports are 6½ feet high, a little less than 15 inches front to back, and 4 feet apart. The shelves are 8-foot pine 1-by-12s.

The supports can be shorter and — if the shelves are cut from 1-by-10s or 1-by-

8s — shallower. Because the width of the boards may vary by as much as ⅛ inch, measure each one at both ends and in the middle; then construct the ladders wide enough to accommodate the widest shelf. If the shelves will hold books or other heavy items, the two supports should be no more than 3 feet apart. If need be, the shelves can be as short as 4 feet. Lightly loaded shelves may be 10 feet long, with the supports set 5 feet apart.

Building the assembly consists chiefly of cutting the pieces and attaching them with glue, nails and screws. A lumber-yard will saw the wood, but it costs less to cut the wood at home with a miter box and backsaw. As the batches are cut, stack them in separate piles. Labeling the pieces is not essential, but a perfect fit is crucial: The best way to achieve it is to set up a particleboard-and-lath jig (Step 1).

After drilling the pilot holes for attaching the shelves, sand all exposed surfaces with medium (100-grit), then fine (150-grit) sandpaper, and apply a sealer. The supports and shelves can then be finished with three coats of an oil-based satin or mat enamel. Avoid high-gloss finishes; they reveal imperfections in the wood.

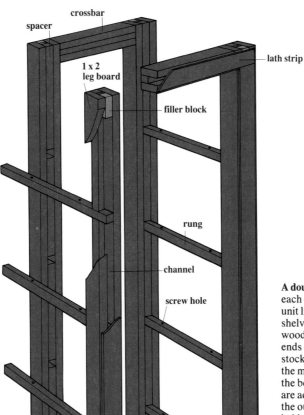

A double-ladder shelf unit. Supporting each end of every shelf is a double-ladder unit like this one. The rungs on which the shelves rest are anchored in legs built of wood layers: Vertical spacers and the ends of the rungs between them are molding stock sandwiched by 1-by-2s. Because the molding stock is only half the width of the boards, filler blocks and lath strips are added to conceal the empty channel on the outside edge of each leg. Linking the ladders securely are top and bottom cross-bars that are assembled as the legs are and parallel the shelves.

Materials List

1 x 12	40 ′ clear pine 1 x 12, cut into 5 shelves, 8 ′ long
1 x 2	115 ′ clear pine 1 x 2, cut into: 16 leg boards, 77¼ ″ long 2 crossbar supports, 72 ″ long
Lath	58 ′ lath, ¼ ″ x 1¾ ″, cut into: 8 leg-trim strips, 73½ ″ long 8 crossbar-trim strips, 12¼ ″ long
Molding stock	82 ′ molding stock, ¾ ″ x ¾ ″, cut into: 20 rungs, 14⅜ ″ long 8 spacers, 12⅞ ″ long 40 spacers, 12⅛ ″ long 16 filler blocks, 2 ″ long 1 crossbar support, 6 ′ long
Fasteners	3 3-oz. boxes 16-gauge brads, 1¼ ″ long ½ lb. fourpenny finishing nails 40 No. 8 wood screws, 1¼ ″ long
Finish	oil-based sealer oil-based enamel
For the jig	1 piece ⅝-inch particleboard, 2½ ′ x 8′ 15 ′ lath, ¼ ″ x 1¾ ″, cut into: 2 sidepieces, 78 ″ long 1 crosspiece, 18 ″ long

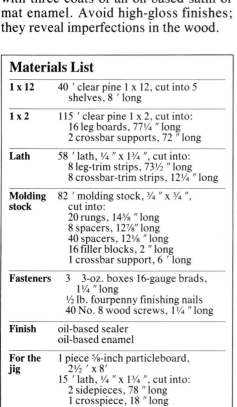

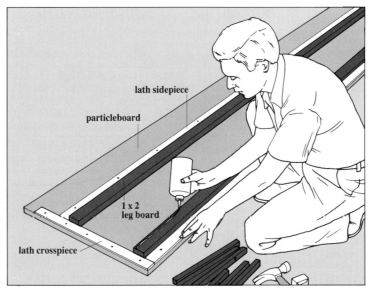

1 **Starting a ladder.** Prepare the rungs by drilling screw holes 3/16 inch in diameter through them 4 inches from each end. Make a jig as shown on page 47, Steps 1 and 2, positioning the sidepieces of lath so that the distance between their inside edges is 14⅜ inches. Butt the ends of a pair of 77¼-inch 1-by-2 leg boards against the lath crosspiece at the top of the jig and align their outside edges with the lath sidepieces. These will become the bottom layers in the ladder sandwich. Apply a thin line of wood glue about 13 inches long to the top of each leg board, ⅜ inch from the inside edge (above). ▶

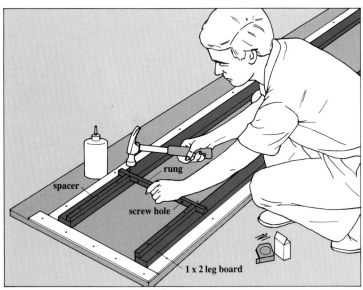

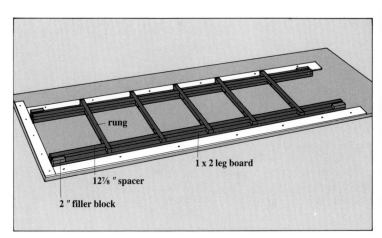

2 **Attaching spacers and rungs.** Place a 12⅛-inch spacer on each glue line, adjusting the spacers to sit flush with the end and the inside edge of each leg board. Anchor each spacer by driving in 1¼-inch-long 16-gauge finishing brads at the middle and 2 inches from the ends. Wipe away any glue seepage with a damp cloth. Spread thin glue lines crosswise on both leg boards ⅜ inch below the ends of the spacers. Place a rung across the jig from leg board to leg board, with the holes in the rung facing the top and bottom of the ladder and the rung butted tightly against the ends of the spacers. Align the ends of the rung with the outside edges of the leg boards. Nail the rung to each leg by driving a 1¼-inch brad through it ¾ inch from each end *(above)*.

3 **Completing the middle layer.** Attach four more pairs of 12⅛-inch spacers, separating each pair with a rung and butting all of the pieces tightly against one another as you did in Step 2. Glue and nail a final pair of spacers — choosing the ones that are 12⅞ inches long — to what will be the top end of each leg. Then apply a 2-inch-long glue line along the outside edge of both ends of each leg and set 2-inch filler blocks in the glue, aligning the blocks with the edges of the leg boards. Secure the blocks to the leg boards by driving finishing brads through each end of the blocks.

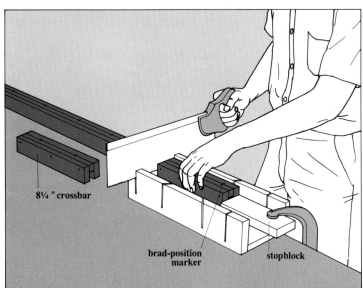

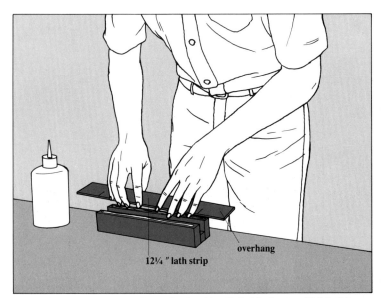

6 **Making the crossbars.** Lay a 72-inch-long 1-by-2 on the worktable. Apply a glue line ⅜ inch from the edge of one wide face of the 1-by-2. Position the 72-inch strip of molding stock on the glue so that one edge aligns with the edge of the 1-by-2. Nail the molding to the 1-by-2 with brads 4 inches apart. Mark the position of each brad with a pencil on the outward-facing edge to forestall damaging a saw blade when you cut this assembly into crossbars. Attach the other 72-inch 1-by-2 to the top of the molding with glue and fourpenny nails at 4-inch intervals. Let the glue dry overnight. Clamp a stopblock in a miter box 8¼ inches from one 90° slot, butt the sandwiched assembly against the block and cut eight 8¼-inch crossbars *(above)*, avoiding the pencil marks and nails.

7 **Attaching lath to crossbars.** On the side of a ladder leg to which lath is attached, measure the distance from the edge of the lath to the far edge of the leg — about 2 inches. Multiply by two and add 8¼ inches. Using 1¾-inch-wide lath, cut eight strips to this measurement — about 12¼ inches. Make tick marks on each cut lath strip as far from each end as the leg width just measured. Turn a crossbar channel side up and apply a thin glue line along the narrow face of each 1-by-2. Using the marks on the lath strip as a guide, center the lath on the crossbar *(above)* so that the overhangs at each end are the same length. Nail the lath to the crossbar with finishing brads 4 inches apart on both sides of the channel. Attach the remaining lath strips to the seven other crossbars.

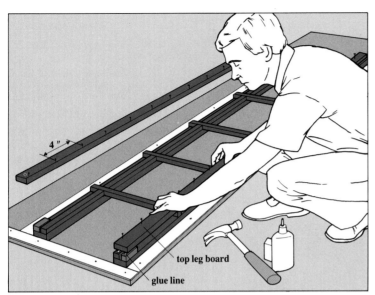

4 **Attaching the top leg boards.** Start fourpenny finishing nails at 4-inch intervals along two 77¼-inch 1-by-2s, ⅜ inch from their inner edges. On one side of the ladder, apply a thin glue line down the center of the spacers and filler blocks and on the rung ends. Lay one of the prepared legs on top of the glue line *(above)*, aligning it with the pieces beneath at the inside edge and the top end. Drive in the nails, correcting the leg's alignment as you go. Attach the other top leg board in the same way and let the glue dry overnight. Then, if necessary, trim the bottom end of each leg. Sand the top and bottom ends of both legs with medium (100-grit) sandpaper. Build three more ladders of the same dimensions.

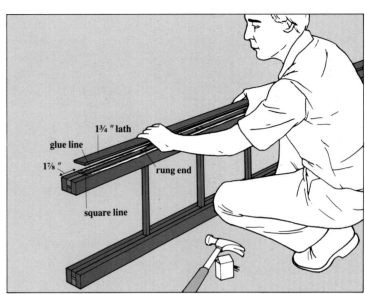

5 **Adding lath.** Turn one ladder on its side. Measure 1⅞ inches from each end on the side of the uppermost leg and make tick marks. Draw a square line across the side at each mark, measure the distance between the lines and cut a 1¾-inch-wide lath strip to that length. Apply a long, thin glue line from one line to the other along the top edges of both leg boards. Also squeeze a dot of glue onto each rung end. Center the lath on the leg *(above)* so the ends of the lath meet the pencil lines and it leaves a ¼-inch reveal along each side. Attach the lath with brads 4 inches apart along both leg boards. Recess the brads with a nail set *(page 33, Step 11);* fill the indentations with wood putty and let it dry overnight. Add lath to the other side and to the three other ladders.

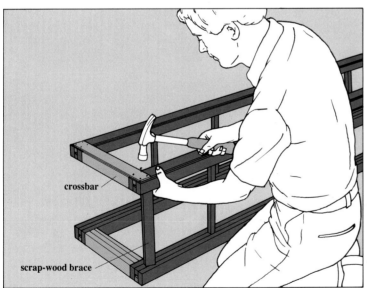

8 **Joining pairs of ladders.** Lay two ladders on their sides, parallel to each other. Apply lines of glue to both ends of a crossbar (shown here in a lighter tint) and to the underside of the lath overhangs. Lower the crossbar into place between the ends of two legs, butting the overhangs tightly against the ends of the lath nailed to the legs. Press the outside edges of the legs against the ends of the crossbar to help the glue adhere. Brace the ends of the legs with scrap wood and nail the lath overhangs to each leg with four finishing brads. Attach the seven other crossbars in the same way. Let the glue dry overnight. Then sand all of the exposed surfaces and the shelves with fine (150-grit) paper; apply a coat of sealer and three coats of satin-finish oil-based enamel.

9 **Fastening shelves to rungs.** Stand the two double units upright, with the 12⅞-inch spacers at the top and the units 4 feet apart. At both ends of each shelf, measure for an even overhang and mark the board with masking tape. Carefully slide a shelf onto the top rungs. Using the tapes as a guide, center the shelf lengthwise and crosswise between the pairs of ladders. Insert an awl through the rung holes to mark pilot-hole positions on the shelf. Remove the shelf and drill ½-inch-deep pilot holes at each mark. Reposition the shelf, aligning the shelf and rung holes. Insert 1¼-inch wood screws through the rungs and drive them into the bottom of the shelf. Attach the bottom shelf the same way, then — with the unit stabilized — attach the three remaining shelves.

Wood slabs that seem to float

Suspended free, the shelves below produce a spare, uncluttered wall treatment. Their supports are invisible but sturdy: Each shelf is held aloft by two rods projecting from the wall into holes drilled in the shelf.

The shelves can be arranged in virtually any pattern on any wall where rods can be driven at least 3 inches into solid material. With a wood-frame plaster or wallboard wall, the rods can be sunk deep into studs. Brick and some modern adobe construction also provide secure support;

follow the steps here, setting the support rods at 16-inch intervals, using a masonry bit, and anchoring the rods with epoxy. Walls of stone or cement block and walls with metal studs, however, are inappropriate for this form of shelving.

With wood-frame walls, each shelf must be at least 20 inches long (to cross two studs) and no more than 40 inches long. It can project up to a foot beyond each stud. The rods must be sunk into the exact centers of studs. Locate them by the technique described on page 21,

working along a level, horizontal line so that your measurements remain constant.

You can mark stud positions and the horizontal guideline with chalk (opposite) or by tacking string to the wall. Chalk is quick to apply but difficult to remove. To test your wall, make a chalk mark in an inconspicuous place, then wash it away. If a stain remains, either use string and tacks or plan to repaint or repaper the wall after you have installed the rods.

Minor repairs and touch-up painting will be needed to conceal the exploratory

holes that verify the location of each stud center. To minimize repairs, plan shelf placement on graph paper, then apply strips of drafting tape to the wall to represent each shelf. The tape, available at art-supply stores, will not mar the wall.

For strength, use ⅜-inch steel rods, threaded as here or plain, cut to measure at a hardware store. The rods must extend nearly halfway into the shelf and 3 inches or more into the wall. To hold such big rods, the shelves must be solid boards at least 1¾ inches thick — of either hardwood or softwood. For stability, they should be no deeper than 10 inches.

To make sure that each shelf sits properly against the wall, emphasize to the lumberyard or millwork the importance of planing the wood accurately. Before you accept the lumber, check each piece with a square to see if its top surface and back edge meet at a 90° angle.

For the shelves to be level, all holes must be drilled perfectly straight. Use a drill guide (page 124) to keep the bit from swerving off line. When drilling deeply into studs, beware of pipes and electric cables. If you should hit pipe or cable, stop immediately and call a plumber or an electrician. After drilling the shelves, finish them with paint or varnish. First, sand with medium (100-grit), then fine (150-grit) sandpaper. For a natural, rustic look, finish with penetrating oil, or with wood stain and varnish, sanding between coats with very fine (220-grit) paper. For a glossy look, apply a sealer and finish with several coats of oil-based enamel.

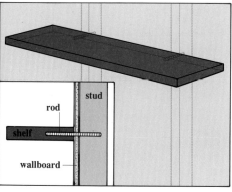

Concealed support. Holes drilled in wall studs hide the steel rods that anchor apparently floating shelves. The solid wood shelves are heavyweights: 1¾ inches thick, 8 inches deep and 30 inches wide. The rods are ⅜ inch in diameter and extend 3½ inches into both the studs and the shelves, as seen here in cross section.

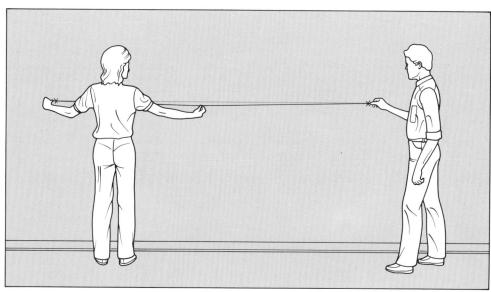

1 Snapping a horizontal chalk line. Using a tape measure and chalk, mark two points, 4½ feet from the floor at the left and right ends of the planned shelf area. Have a helper hold the end of a chalk line at one mark (or tack the end at that mark). Stretch the line to the opposite mark and hold it taut with one hand. Use your other hand to pluck the line out from the wall, then let it go. It will snap sharply back, leaving a line on the wall.

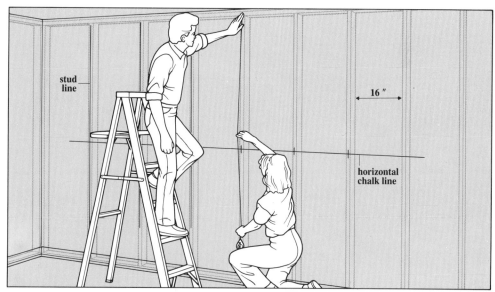

2 Marking the stud positions. Working from left to right along the horizontal chalk line, find and mark the centers of the first two studs in the shelf area (page 21). Measure between the two marks, then repeat that measurement along the line, marking the presumed location of each stud center. (You will confirm the centers in Step 4.) Use the chalk line as a plumb bob: Have a helper hold the end of the string 7 feet high, with the string crossing the stud center mark and the locked case hanging loose. Snap a vertical chalk line there (above) and repeat at each stud. ▶

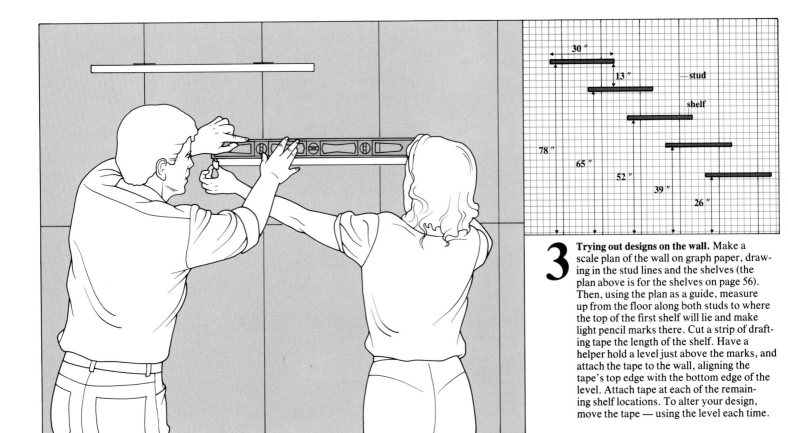

3 **Trying out designs on the wall.** Make a scale plan of the wall on graph paper, drawing in the stud lines and the shelves (the plan above is for the shelves on page 56). Then, using the plan as a guide, measure up from the floor along both studs to where the top of the first shelf will lie and make light pencil marks there. Cut a strip of drafting tape the length of the shelf. Have a helper hold a level just above the marks, and attach the tape to the wall, aligning the tape's top edge with the bottom edge of the level. Attach tape at each of the remaining shelf locations. To alter your design, move the tape — using the level each time.

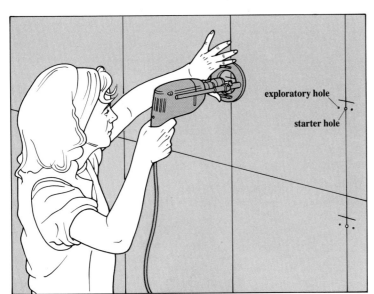

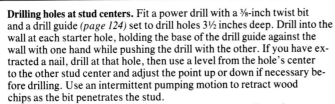

5 **Drilling holes at stud centers.** Fit a power drill with a ⅜-inch twist bit and a drill guide (page 124) set to drill holes 3½ inches deep. Drill into the wall at each starter hole, holding the base of the drill guide against the wall with one hand while pushing the drill with the other. If you have extracted a nail, drill at that hole, then use a level from the hole's center to the other stud center and adjust the point up or down if necessary before drilling. Use an intermittent pumping motion to retract wood chips as the bit penetrates the stud.

Insert a ⅜-inch steel rod into each hole. Clean the wall, apply spackling compound to the exploratory holes and let it dry overnight. Smooth the spackle with fine (150-grit) sandpaper, then paint over it.

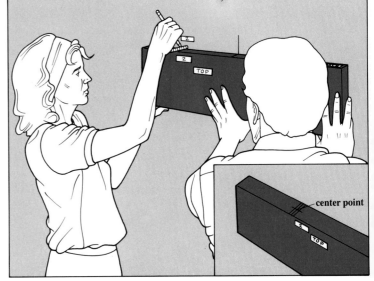

6 **Marking the shelf for drilling.** Using pieces of drafting tape as labels, mark each shelf and its location on the wall with corresponding numbers. Label the top surface and back edge of each shelf with tape. At the wall, mark the center point between a pair of rods. Mark the center of the back edge of a shelf. Have a helper hold the shelf flat against the wall, aligning the center of its back edge with the mark on the wall. Draw lines along the sides of the rods onto the back edge of the shelf (above). Take the shelf down and use a ruler to locate the center point between each pair of lines (inset). Similarly mark the remaining shelves, finishing all the work on one shelf before proceeding to the next.

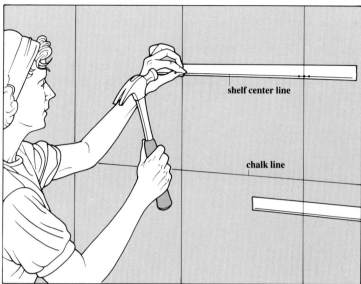

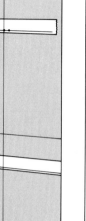

shelf center line

chalk line

Extracting a Nail from a Stud

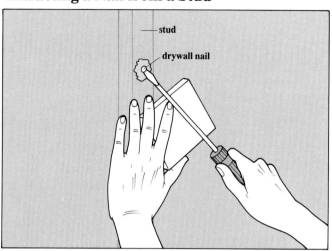

stud

drywall nail

When driving in a nail to produce a starter hole, you may strike a drywall nail used to fasten wallboard to a stud. To remove the nail, use the tip of a screwdriver to scrape away the thin layer of joint compound covering the nailhead. Slide the screwdriver blade beneath the nailhead and, using a wood scrap for leverage, pry the nail partially free. Then use pliers or the claw of a hammer to pull out the nail.

4 **Making starter holes.** Using the level as a straightedge, pencil a horizontal line representing the center line of the back edge of the shelf along each strip of drafting tape. The line will not be centered on the tape unless the tape and the shelf are the same thickness.

With pencil, continue each vertical chalk line across the tape. Then, using the cross points for reference and tapping in a fourpenny finishing nail as a probe, find the exact center of each stud *(page 21)* at the point where the horizontal line on the tape crosses it. With a fourpenny finishing nail and a hammer, tap a ½-inch-deep starter hole at each stud center point. If you happen to hit a nail already in the stud, extract it *(box, right)*. Remove the pieces of tape.

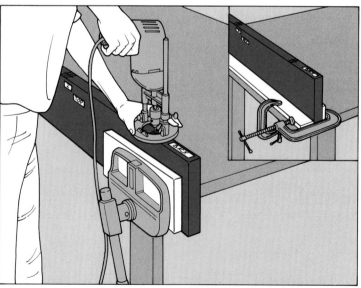

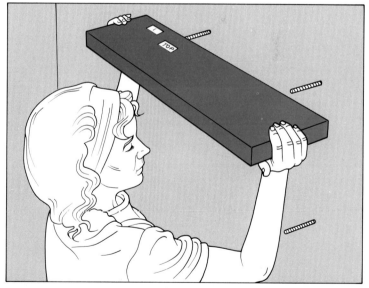

7 **Drilling the holes in the shelf.** At the worktable, secure a shelf, marked edge upward, in a vise, using two pieces of scrap wood to protect the shelf's surfaces. Then, with the same ⅜-inch bit you used on the wall and with the drill guide still set for 3½ inches, drill straight through each center point, using an occasional pumping motion to retract wood chips. Drill identical holes in the remaining shelves. Lacking a vise, secure the shelf between two sturdy pieces of wood, using a 6-inch C clamp to hold the three pieces of lumber together and a 3-inch C clamp to hold one of the supporting pieces to the table *(inset)*.

8 **Fitting the shelf over the rods.** Sand and finish the shelves, keeping them in numbered order so that later you can readily match them to their positions on the wall. After the shelves have dried, fit each one onto the wall, carefully placing first one hole over a rod, then the other. Push the shelf until the back is flush with the wall.

Surrounding a window with books

These bookshelves do more than utilize every scrap of space around the window; they also transform an otherwise plain wall into an intriguing decorative feature. And though they present themselves as a work of polished craftsmanship, you can construct the shelves without using any special tools or joinery skills at all.

The secret of this project's simplicity is that its elements are stacked one atop the other. The shelves — except for some adjustable ones alongside the window that hang on brackets — rest on short vertical supports that in turn stand on shelves below. This eliminates the need for complicated joints such as dadoes. Apart from some fasteners that anchor several of the boards to the walls, only finishing nails, carpenter's glue and (in some cases) a few screws are necessary

to hold the structure together. And it is made of pine boards of only three sizes: 1-by-12, 1-by-3 and 1-by-2. Ask the dealer for wood graded Clear, or Select, and planed on four sides.

The Materials List offers guidelines for estimating how much lumber you need. They are for a bookcase with the same configuration as this one. You may need to modify the plan, however, to fit your wall. A shelf should not span much more than 42 inches, so you may have to use more vertical supports. If so, add them when calculating the amount of lumber.

Also bear in mind that boards range in length from 8 to 20 feet, in 2-foot increments. In figuring the lengths needed, allow a few extra inches for trimming off a board's split ends. If some of your shelves need to be, say, 11 feet long, make clear to the dealer that you require 12-foot-long 1-by-12s. And check the boards' width by stacking them. All 1-by-12s should be about 11¼ inches wide; a board wider than the rest can keep the

structure from fitting together properly. Each upright support must be truly vertical and aligned with supports above and below it. You can accomplish this easily by using what carpenters call a story pole, a guide for marking repetitive measurements — in this case, the places on horizontal boards where the vertical boards should intersect them. Step 1 explains how to make a story pole out of a 1-by-2; you can later incorporate it in the bookcase as a facing board.

Do not attempt to cut the boards ahead of time; measure for them as construction progresses. Take both front and back measurements for wide boards that extend from side wall to side wall, and cut to the shorter figure; resulting small gaps will be hidden when the bookcase is completed. You can use a hand-held crosscut saw, but a circular saw or table saw will make the job go faster. If there is baseboard or molding on the walls where the bookcase is to be built, remove it *(page 67)* before starting the project.

Materials List

1 x 12	5 clear pine 1 x 12s, each at least 4 inches longer than the wall's width. Additional clear pine 1 x 12s equal in total length to 3 times the wall's width and 7 times its height, plus 10 per cent for wastage
1 x 3	11 clear pine 1 x 3s: 4 at least 4 inches longer than the wall's width, 7 at least 4 inches longer than the wall's height
1 x 2	2 clear pine 1 x 2s, both at least 4 inches longer than the wall's height, one of them as long as the wall is wide
Hardware	1 lb. sixpenny finishing nails ½ lb. fourpenny finishing nails 24 wall fasteners *(see Step 7)* 6 No. 10 flat-head wood screws, 2 inches long, if needed *(see Step 11)* bracket pins, 4 for each adjustable shelf

Bookshelves around a window. A base that stretches from side wall to side wall supports the whole structure, including 1-by-3 furring strips that are fastened to each side wall and that rise to the ceiling. The two shelves between the base and the window reach all the way across the unit, resting on short vertical supports. (The vertical supports on the sides are nailed to the furring strips; the others, some of them doubled, are nailed to the shelves above and below.) Along both sides of the window, much longer vertical supports hold adjustable shelves on bracket pins that fit into holes drilled in the supports. Another fixed shelf spans the whole unit above the window, and a top board is added just beneath the ceiling so the vertical lines of the supports will continue up the wall. Horizontal and vertical facing boards on the front of the unit hide the joints of supports and shelves and thus disguise the extremely simple construction of the bookcase.

1 x 3 facing board

1 x 3 facing boards

1 x 12 adjustable shelf

bracket pin

doubled 1 x 12 vertical support

1 x 12 vertical support

1 x 12 fixed shelf

1 x 12

1 x 3 furring strips

1 x 2 facing board

1 x 3

1 x 3s

1 x 2 facing board

1 x 3

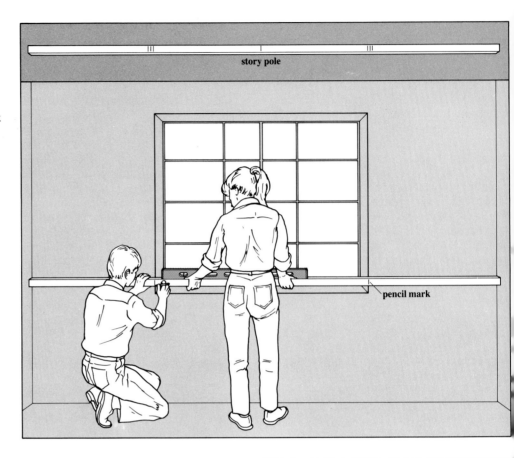

story pole

pencil mark

1 **Making a story pole.** Measure the distance between the two side walls — across the back wall and again about 12 inches out from the back wall — and cut a 1-by-2 to the shorter length. Use a carpenter's square and a pencil to mark a line across the midpoint of the board's face, perpendicular to its edges. Hold the board with a carpenter's level atop it across the window, its midpoint at the window's midpoint. When the board is level, have a helper mark where it crosses the outside edge of the window trim on both sides. Then use the square to draw lines perpendicular to the board's edges at those marks, and at points ¾ inch and 1½ inches outside those marks. The resulting story pole (inset) will serve as a pattern for marking shelves, indicating where they are intersected by vertical supports. If your shelves will be so long that they need more vertical supports, mark those positions, too, on the pole.

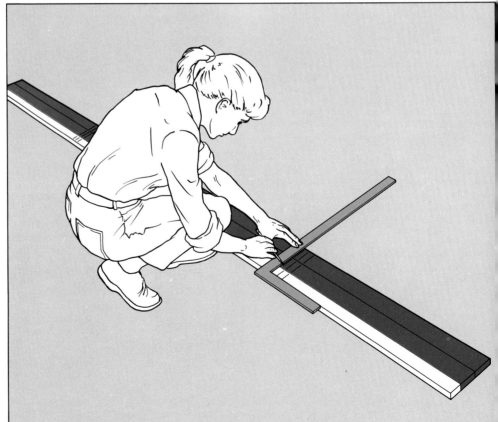

3 **Using the story pole.** Cut two 1-by-3s to the length of the story pole. Lay them flat alongside the pole and align the ends of all three boards, as shown at right. Extend the lines on the story pole across the faces of the 1-by-3s with a pencil and a square.
　　Start a pair of sixpenny finishing nails ½ inch from each end of one of the 1-by-3s. Start two more nails along the center line of each set of three lines on that board, and another pair on the line at the board's center.

2 **Beginning the base.** Near the bottom of the back wall, find and mark the locations of the studs *(page 21)*. Cut a 1-by-3 and a 1-by-12 to the same length as the story pole. Lay the 1-by-12 flat on the floor, its rear edge against the back wall, as a temporary support for the narrower board. Set the 1-by-3 on edge on top of the 1-by-12 and push it flat against the wall. Start some sixpenny finishing nails into the 1-by-3, centering them on the studs. Slipping shims under the 1-by-3 if necessary, level that board *(left)* and nail it in place with two nails in each stud. Now remove the 1-by-12.

1 x 12

1 x 3

4 **Building the base.** Measure the actual width of the 1-by-12 you cut in Step 2 (it should be about 11¼ inches wide) and subtract the combined actual thicknesses of the 1-by-3s cut in Step 3 (probably 1½ inches: ¾ inch each). Use the result — a figure close to 9¾ inches — as the exact length to cut five 1-by-3 crosspieces (called spreaders) for the base, cutting them from one of the wall-height 1-by-3s.

Arrange the five spreaders and the board with the started nails on edge as seen at left. Bracing the spreaders against the board mounted on the wall, drive the nails into the ends of the spreaders. Turn the assembly over, and nail the other marked 1-by-3 to the other ends of the spreaders. If necessary, use shims to level the whole base unit, side to side and front to back. To make sure it is correctly positioned, lay the 1-by-12 cut in Step 2 on it; the top of that board should be flush with the top edge of the 1-by-3 that is nailed to the wall. Then remove the 1-by-12 and nail the base unit securely to the wall-mounted board, using one sixpenny nail every 8 inches. ▶

spreader

5 **Securing the bottom shelf.** Using the story pole as a guide and a carpenter's square to make the lines perpendicular to the edge, mark the positions for vertical supports across the face of the 1-by-12 sawed in Step 2. Next, run a line of glue along the top edges of the two 1-by-3s that form the front and rear of the base (not the 1-by-3 that is nailed to the wall). Lay the 1-by-12, marked face up, on the base and butt its rear edge against the wall-mounted 1-by-3. Drive four evenly spaced sixpenny nails through the shelf into each of the spreaders underneath it: Position the nails no more than ½ inch from each side wall, in the center line of each set of three lines, and in the line across the midpoint of the board.

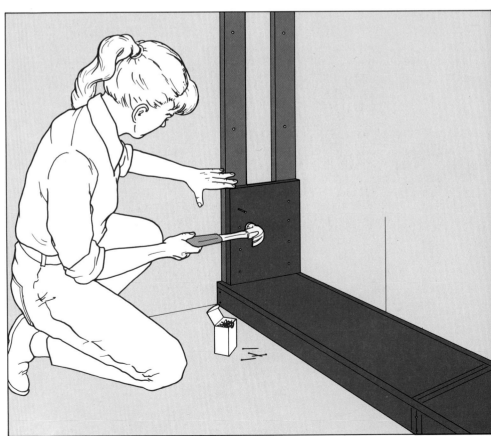

7 **Installing the second shelf.** Measure from the face of the bottom shelf to the bottom of the window frame. Divide by two and subtract ¾ inch: The result is the height of vertical supports that will evenly space the three shelves below the window. Cut seven pieces of 1-by-12 to that length. Position one of these vertical supports at each end of the base shelf and fix it in place by driving four evenly spaced sixpenny nails through it into each furring strip *(right)*.

To determine the length of the second shelf, measure between the faces of the front furring strips and again between the faces of the rear furring strips. Cut the 1-by-12 shelf to the shorter length. Find the midpoint of the shelf's length and align it with the story pole's midpoint. Use a carpenter's square to extend the pole's lines across both faces of the 1-by-12. Run glue along the tops of the vertical supports, position the shelf on the supports and secure it with sixpenny nails at each end.

6 **Putting up furring strips.** Measure from the face of the bottom shelf to the ceiling and cut four 1-by-3s to that length. Along the center line of each, drill six evenly spaced ³⁄₁₆-inch holes through the board and countersink them with a ³⁄₈-inch bit *(page 124)*. The holes will suit whatever fasteners you need to fix these furring strips to the walls *(page 125)*. Use 2-inch No. 10 wood screws in wood studs. In masonry, use the same screws with anchors. Use 3-inch-long ³⁄₁₆-inch toggle bolts for a hollow wall.

Position two furring strips on each side wall, one at the back of the base and the other ¾ inch back from the front edge of the base. Use a level along their side edges to make them plumb in their side-to-side plane. Mark fastener locations on the wall, drill the required holes and start — but do not tighten — the fasteners. Then use the level on the faces of the strips to make sure they are plumb in their front-to-back planes, slipping shims behind them, if necessary *(left)*. Now tighten the fasteners.

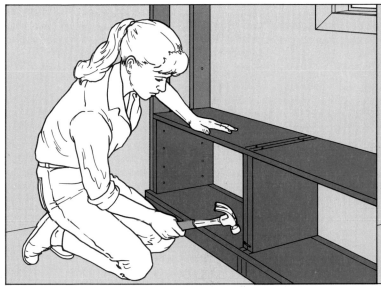

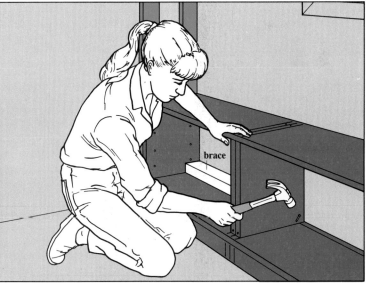

8 **Inserting vertical supports.** Slide a pair of the vertical supports that you cut in Step 7 between the base and second shelf, below one side of the window; align their top and bottom edges with the guidelines drawn on the shelves. Drive two sixpenny nails through the second shelf into the top edge of each support. Then, using fourpenny finishing nails, toenail each support from the front *(above, left)* — that is, drive a nail diagonally through the support's front edge into the shelf below. Next, cut a piece of scrap wood so it will fit snugly between the outermost vertical support of the pair just inserted and the vertical support at the end of the shelf. Use it to brace the pair of supports while you toenail with fourpenny nails from the other side near the rear of the shelf

(above, right). Cutting other scrap-wood braces as necessary, install the other vertical supports, nailing them from the top with sixpenny nails and toenailing them from both sides and the front with fourpenny nails. Center a single support on the midpoint lines of the shelves.

Now measure from the face of the second shelf to the bottom of the window frame, subtract ¾ inch, and cut seven vertical supports for the third shelf to that length. (Theoretically, the size will be the same as that of the supports just installed, but measuring again eliminates the possibility of error.) Following the procedures in Step 7 and this step, install the third shelf and its supports. ▶

9 **Making adjustable shelf supports.** Measure from the face of the third shelf to the top of the window frame. Cut six 1-by-12s to that length. Follow the instructions given in Step 7 on page 31 to drill holes in four of the 1-by-12s for bracket pins to hold adjustable shelves. Be sure to mark the bottom ends of the boards so the holes will be aligned when the boards are installed. Stand one of these drilled boards on the third shelf against a side wall, and nail it to the furring strips, using five evenly spaced sixpenny nails in each strip *(right)*. Nail another drilled board to the furring strips on the other side wall.

Next, measure, cut, mark, glue and nail down the fourth shelf — over the top of the window frame — following the procedure in Step 7. Insert doubled vertical supports under this shelf on each side of the window — drilled boards facing their drilled mates on the side walls, and undrilled boards behind them, next to the window frame. While a helper holds them, nail them into place from above and with toenails as described in Step 8.

12 **Adding facing boards.** With sixpenny nails, attach a 1-by-3 cut to fit wall to wall across the front of the top board, its upper edge butting against the ceiling. Cut two 1-by-3s and two 1-by-2s to fit between its bottom edge and the face of the bottom shelf (use the story pole as one of the 1-by-2s). With glue and sixpenny nails, attach the 1-by-3s flat against the edges of the furring strips, their outside edges butting against the side walls. Then use glue and sixpenny nails to fix the two 1-by-2s to the edges of the doubled vertical supports. If there is a gap under the base of the bookcase, hide it with quarter-round molding nailed to the base with 1-inch 16-gauge brads.

Next, set visible nails *(page 33, Step 11)* and cover them and the screwheads with wood putty. Cut adjustable shelves ⅛ inch shorter than the distance between their supports. Sand the bookcase with medium (100-grit) sandpaper, then with fine (150-grit) sandpaper, and finish with either an oil-based sealer and enamel or an appropriate sealer and latex enamel. Then install the bracket pins and adjustable shelves.

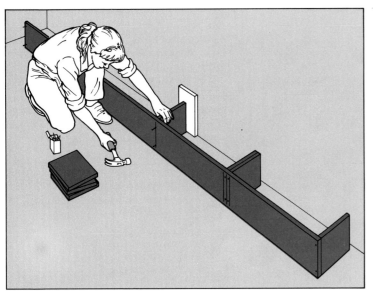

10 **Constructing the upper assembly.** Measure across the ceiling from the face of each furring strip on one side wall to the corresponding strip on the opposite wall. Cut a 1-by-12 to the shorter measurement. Mark both of its faces with the story-pole lines.

Measure from the face of the fourth shelf to the ceiling, subtract 1½ inches, and cut seven 1-by-12s to that length. Start pairs of sixpenny nails ½ inch from each end of the long board, between the lines of each triple-line set and along the midpoint line. Brace one of the short 1-by-12s against a wall protected by scrap wood, align it with a pair of nails, and nail the long board to it. Attach the other vertical supports the same way.

11 **Installing the upper assembly.** If the section of the fourth shelf above the window spans more than 42 inches, strengthen the middle of the upper assembly with screws: Avoiding the nails, drill three countersunk pilot holes *(page 124)* for 2-inch No. 10 screws through the long board into the end of the midpoint vertical support; drive the screws. With a helper, place the upper assembly on the fourth shelf *(above)*. Using fourpenny nails, toenail all the vertical supports except the midpoint support. If the span over the window is 42 inches or less, drive a pair of sixpenny finishing nails through the fourth shelf into the midpoint support. If the span is longer, fasten shelf to support with three countersunk screws.

Removing Baseboards and Other Molding

If there is a baseboard in the room where you are putting your bookshelves, you must remove it from the bookcase wall and the side walls before beginning the project. First slit the paint seal between baseboard and wall with a utility knife.

Then — beginning on the bookshelf wall, since that baseboard will not be reinstalled and therefore can be broken — tap the end of a pry bar behind the baseboard. Slip a thin piece of scrap wood behind the bar, both to increase your leverage and to protect the wall. Work along the length of the baseboard, prying it from the wall and inserting shims behind it, until it can be pulled free.

When removing baseboard from the side walls, take care not to break it, since you will have to cut it to fit and reinstall it once the bookshelves are finished. If there is molding in front of the baseboard, remove it first, using the same technique. Any molding at the top of the walls must also be removed to make room for the shelves.

shim

The dramatic beauty of an arch

This gracefully arched alcove, its glass shelves dramatically lit by concealed fixtures, provides a striking focal point in a room's décor. Any similar alcove — whether a niche in the wall or a recess next to a fireplace — can be endowed with the same classic glamor if it does not exceed the size limitations imposed by glass shelving: 4 feet wide by 2 feet deep.

The key pieces in transforming an alcove into a glass-shelved cabinet are four large rectangles of ¾-inch birch plywood: a base shelf, two side-wall panels and an arched façade. All of these can be cut to size by the lumber dealer.

To determine the width of the base shelf, measure across your alcove at baseboard height; for its depth, measure from the front to the back of the alcove and subtract ¾ inch for the bottom facing. For the height of the wall panels, measure from the top of the baseboard to the ceiling and subtract ½ inch; that will leave inconspicuous gaps at the ceiling but will ensure that you can fit the panels in. The width of the panels should equal the alcove's depth minus 1½ inches to allow for facing boards and molding. Measure across the alcove at the ceiling to determine the width of the arch piece; use two thirds of that measurement for its height.

The other wood in the cabinet is narrow stock pine lumber you can cut using a miter box and backsaw. You may also need new baseboard and ceiling molding.

Before you begin, remove the baseboard from the alcove and the adjacent walls; take down the ceiling molding if there is any. Replace them when the cabinet is completed. A 1-by-4 facing provides a nailing surface for the baseboard. Similarly, a spacer fits under the ceiling molding. Here, the spacer is a 1-by-3; you may need wider lumber to accommodate wider ceiling molding.

Narrow decorative molding is attached above the arch and at the top and bottom of the vertical facing boards. Use molding that blends with the room's woodwork; ¾-inch base cap molding is used here.

To ensure a perfect fit for the glass shelves, measure for them after installing the wall panels. Then order shelves cut from ⅜-inch-thick glass; have the edges rounded smooth or beveled. The "eyeball" accent lights are available where lighting supplies are sold. Have them installed by an electrician before you begin.

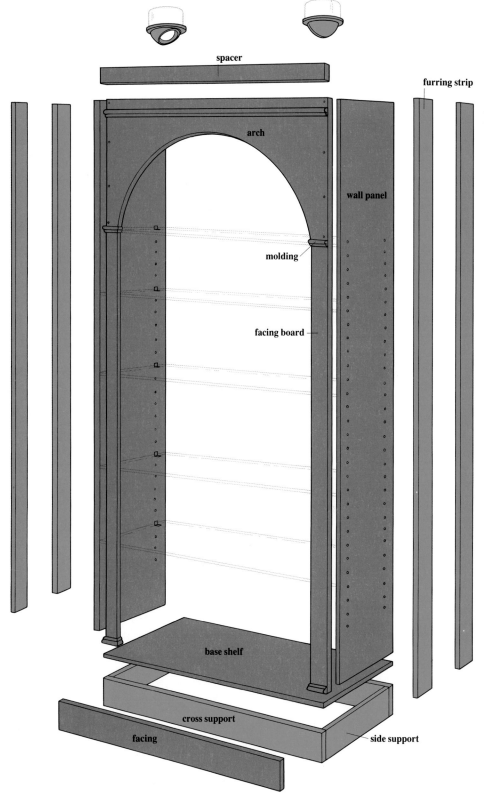

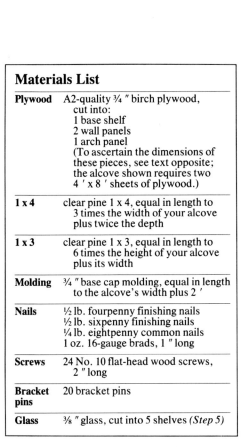

Materials List

Plywood	A2-quality ¾ ″ birch plywood, cut into: 1 base shelf 2 wall panels 1 arch panel (To ascertain the dimensions of these pieces, see text opposite; the alcove shown requires two 4 ′ x 8 ′ sheets of plywood.)
1 x 4	clear pine 1 x 4, equal in length to 3 times the width of your alcove plus twice the depth
1 x 3	clear pine 1 x 3, equal in length to 6 times the height of your alcove plus its width
Molding	¾ ″ base cap molding, equal in length to the alcove's width plus 2 ′
Nails	½ lb. fourpenny finishing nails ½ lb. sixpenny finishing nails ¼ lb. eightpenny common nails 1 oz. 16-gauge brads, 1 ″ long
Screws	24 No. 10 flat-head wood screws, 2 ″ long
Bracket pins	20 bracket pins
Glass	⅜ ″ glass, cut into 5 shelves (Step 5)

An arched alcove. A plywood base shelf rests on 1-by-4 supports fastened to the alcove walls. Two 1-by-3 furring strips run from the base shelf to the ceiling on each side wall; plywood wall panels are screwed to the furring strips. Glass shelves rest on bracket pins inserted into holes drilled in the panels. The plywood arch is glued and nailed to the front edges of the wall panels. Two 1-by-3 vertical facing boards and strips of decorative molding hide plywood edges and joints. A 1-by-3 spacer at the top and a 1-by-4 facing at the bottom, which provide nailing surfaces for the ceiling molding and baseboard, run straight across the front of the alcove. Two accent lights are installed in the ceiling behind the arch.

1 **Marking for the base.** Remove any base-board and ceiling molding from the alcove and along the adjacent wall, following the technique shown in the box on page 67. Mark a point ½ inch down from the height of the former baseboard at the middle of the back wall. Then, using a long carpenter's level as your straightedge, draw a level line across the wall through the mark. Continue the line across the two side walls, using the level in the same fashion.

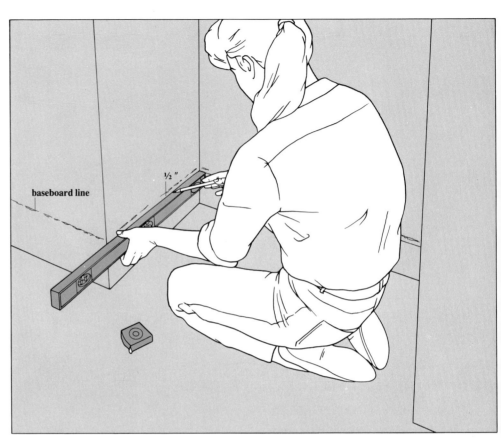

baseboard line

½ "

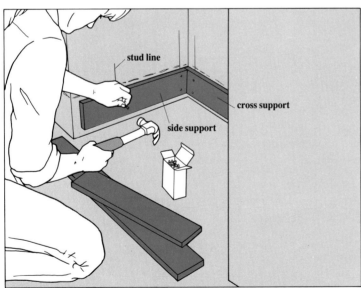

stud line

cross support

side support

2 **Building the base.** Locate and mark the studs *(page 21)* in the back and side walls. Measure across the alcove at floor level, and use a miter box and backsaw to cut two 1-by-4 cross supports that long. Measure from the back to the front of the alcove, subtract 2¼ inches, and cut two 1-by-4 side supports. Hold a cross support against the back wall, its top edge against the line, and nail it to the studs, using two eightpenny common nails per stud. If there are no studs, use the appropriate fasteners for your wall *(page 125)*. Align a side support's top edge with the line on the side wall, butt its end against the back support, and nail it to the studs *(above)*. Repeat on the other side. Nail the front cross support to the ends of the two side supports with two sixpenny finishing nails at each end.

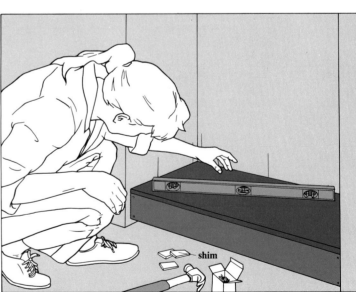

shim

3 **Leveling the base shelf.** Lay the plywood base shelf on the base and check it for levelness. If necessary, insert shims — slender, wedge-shape strips of wood — between the shelf and the base to level the shelf. Then nail the shelf to the base with fourpenny finishing nails spaced 5 inches apart. Set the nails *(page 33, Step 11)*.

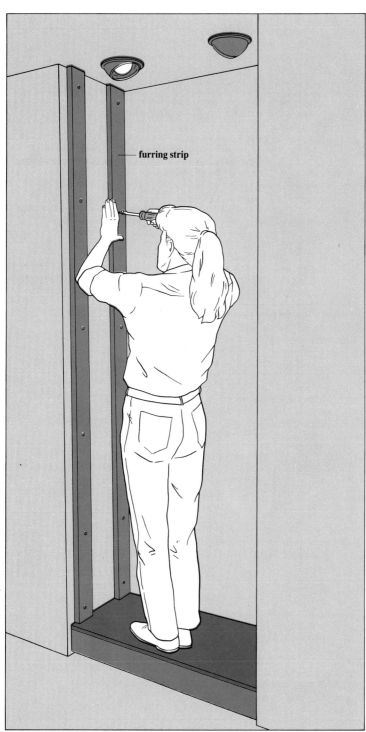

furring strip

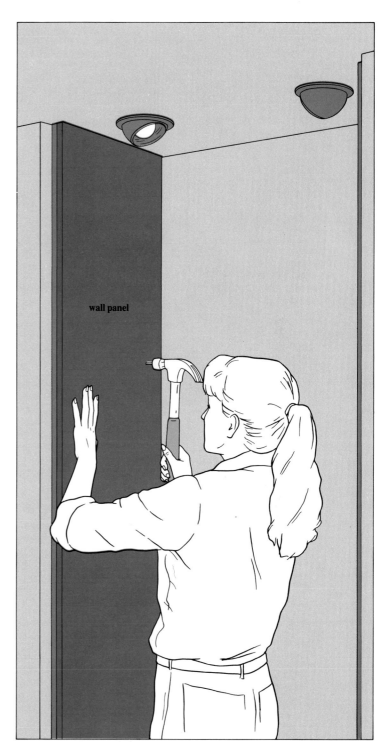

wall panel

4 **Fastening furring strips.** Measure from the bottom shelf to the ceiling of the alcove, then cut four 1-by-3 furring strips to that length. Drill six evenly spaced ¼-inch-diameter holes through each strip, counterbored with a ⅜-inch bit *(page 124)*. Position a strip against the side wall in the back corner of the alcove and use an awl to mark screw positions through the holes. Place a second strip with its front edge ¾ inch from the front of the base shelf. Plumb the strip and mark the position of its screw holes. If there are studs at these marks, drill ⅛-inch pilot holes into the studs at the marks, then attach the furring strips with 2-inch-long No. 10 wood screws, but do not tighten them yet. Lacking studs, use fasteners appropriate for the wall. Repeat for the opposite wall.

5 **Attaching the wall panels.** Use a level to check that furring strips are vertical; insert shims behind them, if necessary, to plumb them. Place one leg of a carpenter's square across the back wall and the other leg across the strips on the side wall; if they are not perpendicular to the wall, square them by more shimming. Now tighten the fasteners. Nail the wall panels to the furring strips with sixpenny finishing nails every 8 inches *(above)*. Set the nails. Measure at 2-foot intervals, front and back, to find the shortest distance between the wall panels; also measure the width of the wall panels. Order glass shelves cut ⅛ inch shorter in each dimension. Note: If the distance between panels varies by more than ¼ inch, pull the wall panels off and readjust the furring strips. ▶

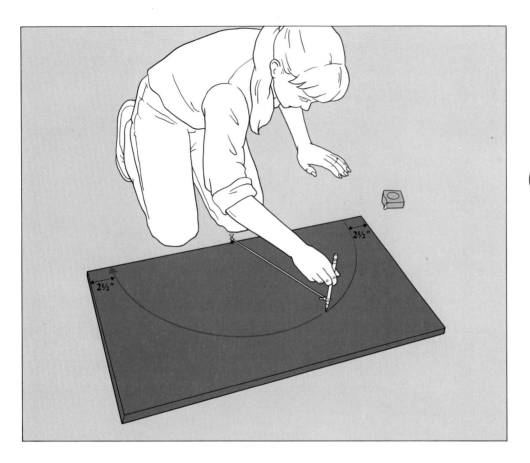

6 **Marking the arch.** Along the bottom of the plywood arch piece, make a pencil mark 2½ inches from each side edge. Drive a sixpenny finishing nail into the board ½ inch above the center of its bottom edge. Tie the end of a piece of nylon twine to the nail, stretch it out to one of the side marks and tie the other end of the twine to a pencil at that point. The taut string should allow the pencil point to rest directly on the mark. Then, beginning at the mark, draw an arc around to the opposite mark, keeping the pencil vertical.

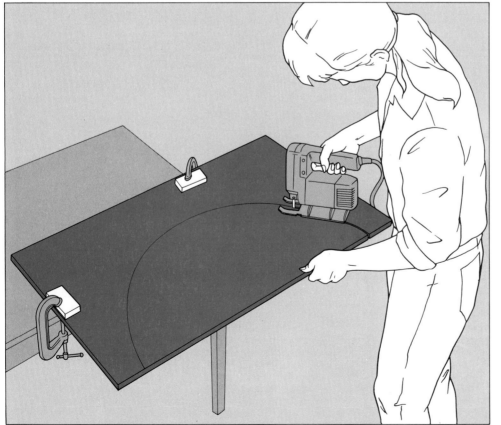

7 **Cutting the arch.** Set the marked plywood on a worktable with one side of the plywood overhanging the edge. Use two C clamps to hold the plywood, inserting wood scraps under the jaws of the clamps to protect the wood's surface. With a saber saw, cut along the marked arch. Shift the board and reclamp it as many times as necessary to complete the cut. Lay the arch on the floor and start fourpenny finishing nails in rows ⅜ inch from each side, spacing the nails at 6-inch intervals.

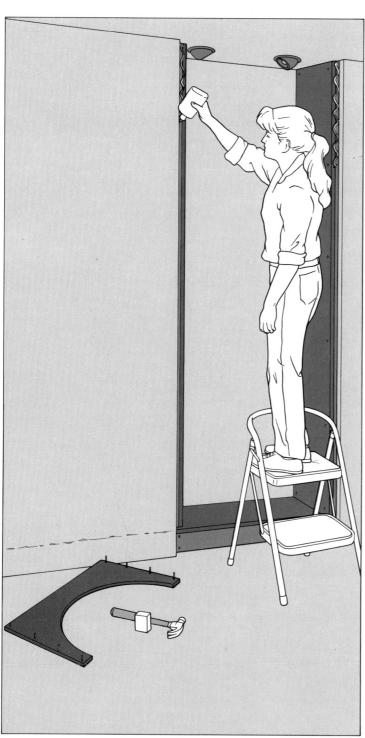

8 **Attaching the arch.** Run a line of glue as long as the side of the arch from the ceiling down the front edge of each wall panel and furring strip. Then have a helper hold the arch across the top of the alcove, butting it against the ceiling. Nail the arch to the edges of the wall panels. Use a nail set to drive the heads of the nails below the surface of the wood.

9 **Making the wall-panel drill jig.** Cut a 1-by-3 long enough to reach from the base shelf to a couple of inches above the bottom of the arch. Hold the 1-by-3 against the side of the alcove just behind the arch. Draw a line across the 1-by-3 where it meets the bottom of the arch and label that end the top. Then lay the 1-by-3 on the floor. Determine and mark the center of its width at several points and connect the marks with a straight line the length of the board. Draw a line across the board 10 inches from its bottom end. Starting at the top line and ending at the bottom one, make pencil marks across the center line every three inches. Put the board on scrap wood and drill ¼-inch holes through it at each mark. ▶

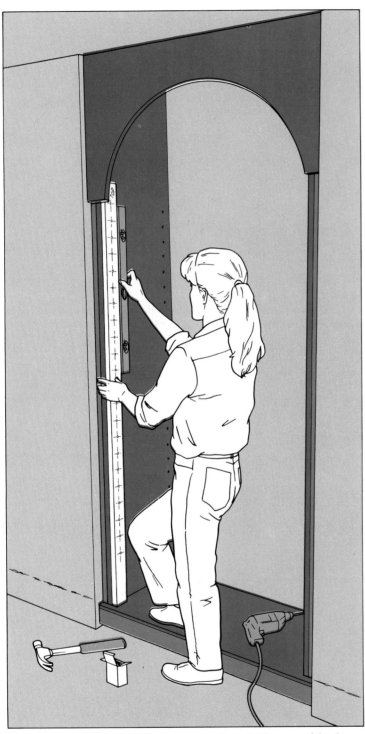

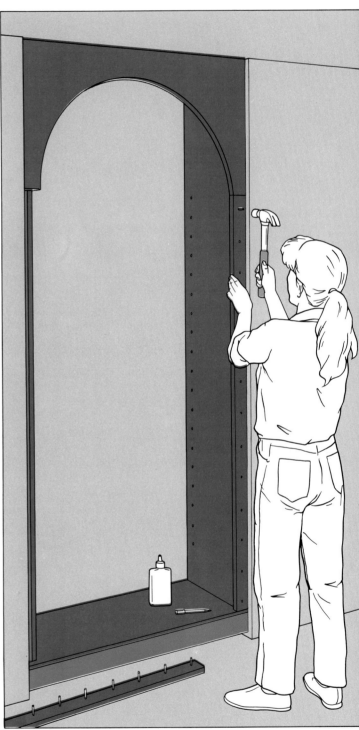

10 **Drilling the panels.** Set the drilling jig in the back corner of the alcove, flat against the wall panel. Make sure the end labeled top is up. Use the level to plumb the jig, then tack the jig to the panel with nails driven in partway at each end and at the middle. Using a ¼-inch bit, drill through the holes in the jig and ½ inch or more into the wall panel. Pull the jig loose and stand it alongside the front edge of the wall panel (*above*). Plumb it, tack it to the panel and drill through the holes. Repeat the process for the opposite wall panel.

11 **Attaching vertical facing.** On each side of the alcove, measure from the bottom shelf to the bottom of the arch. Cut two 1-by-3s to these lengths. Start fourpenny finishing nails spaced 6 inches apart ⅜ inch inside one edge of each 1-by-3. Run a line of wood glue along the front edges of the wall panels and furring strips. Then nail the 1-by-3s to the edges of the furring strips. Set the nails.

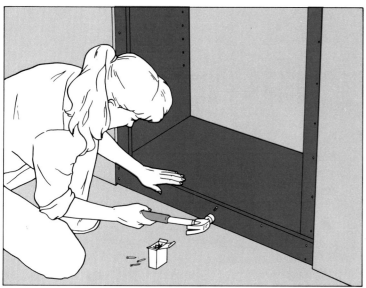

12 **Attaching the bottom facing board.** Measure across the floor at the front of the alcove, between the two side walls. Cut a 1-by-4 to that length. Nail it across the front of the base shelf, its top edge flush with the top surface of the shelf. Use fourpenny finishing nails spaced at 5-inch intervals.

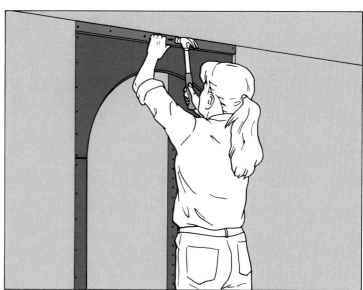

13 **Attaching the top spacer.** Measure across the ceiling between the two side walls at the front of the alcove. Cut a 1-by-3 to that length. Start fourpenny finishing nails down the center of the 1-by-3 spacer, placing them 1½ inches from each end, and 7 to 8 inches apart in between. Next, wedge a piece of scrap 1-by-3 between the arch and the back alcove wall to brace the arch. Hold the spacer across the top of the arch, butted against the ceiling, and secure it by driving in the nails. Cut a strip of base cap molding the same length as the spacer. Nail the molding — its broad curve up — just below the spacer with 1-inch-long 16-gauge brads *(page 33, Step 11)*.

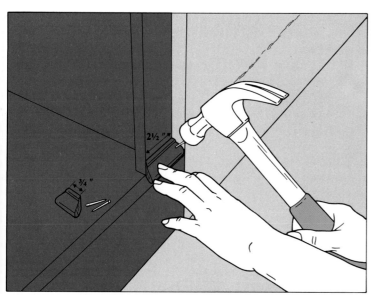

14 **Attaching additional base cap molding.** Use a miter box and a backsaw to cut two molding pieces, each with one end cut at a 90° angle and the other end at a 45° angle to form a mitered corner around the base of the right vertical facing board. One piece should measure 2½ inches along the thin edge, the other ¾ inch, as seen above. (TIP: Hold the strip of molding against the facing board and mark the direction of each angle before you cut it.) Glue the pieces in place, thin edge up, and nail them with 1-inch 16-gauge brads. Cut and attach molding to the bottom of the other vertical facing board. Then cover the joints at the top of the facing boards with molding nailed thin edge down.

15 **Finishing the alcove.** Replace the baseboard and ceiling molding with the old material, or with new strips if needed. Attach the boards with sixpenny finishing nails spaced at 8-inch intervals. After installing the ceiling molding across the top of the alcove, remove the 1-by-3 brace from behind the arch. Use a nail set to recess all nailheads, then putty the holes. After the putty has dried, sand all of the new wood, first with medium (100-grit), then with fine (150-grit) sandpaper. Seal the wood with shellac or other sealer. Paint the alcove with an oil- or latex-based enamel, sanding between coats with very fine (220-grit) paper. Finally, install bracket pins where you want the shelves and set the glass shelves in place.

Cabinets and their hardware

The smallest details of a cabinet can have the greatest effect on its appearance. Handles, hinges and other bits of hardware often provide the most prominent visual cues to a cabinet's character. They can inform a viewer of the cabinet's period style, give an impression of whether it is costly or inexpensive, convey formality or a casual air, and even, sometimes, tattle about whether the owner takes good care of it.

Fortunately for anyone who wants to take advantage of the visual influence of hardware, cabinet fittings are available in almost overwhelming variety. Choices of materials and finishes include, among others, wood, glass, ceramic and plastic, chrome and copper, aluminum, pewter and ersatz pewter, polished brass, brushed brass and antique brass (meaning paint has been brushed onto it, then mostly rubbed off).

Styles range through a dazzling spectrum. Consider just a few of the different forms of hardware you grip to open a drawer: knob, knob with backplate, drop pull with backplate, finger pull, wire pull, bail pull, bail pull with backplate—the list goes on and on.

The pieces of hardware displayed opposite are a small sampling of what can be purchased; these are limited to forms (although not to styles) that are applicable to the cabinet projects on the following pages and to the interchangeable modules in the next section of this book. To familiarize yourself with the whole range of decorative hardware, visit hardware stores, lumberyards and home centers in your area, and consult the catalogues of hardware manufacturers. You may also want to explore books about furniture periods and styles so that you can match appropriate fittings to your cabinet project.

Cabinet hardware falls roughly into three basic categories: handles (which include knobs and pulls); catches and latches; and hinges. The three should complement each other in style and finish on any given cabinet.

Knobs, pulls and other handles are usually the most noticeable decorative elements on doors or drawers and have the most power to define the character of the entire piece. Most knobs and some pulls are attached by machine screws, slipped through holes in the wood from within the cabinet, although some come fixed to a wood screw that you drive into the front of the door or drawer by turning the knob. Many traditional pulls have decorative mounting plates that you screw to the face of the cabinet.

Hinges are made in many configurations designed to hang doors in different ways. One of the most common—the type shown here—is the decorative full-surface hinge. This type is used where the exterior surfaces of the door and the frame are flush; one leaf of the hinge is fixed to the front of the door and the other is attached to the front of the jamb. The full-surface hinge is easy to install, comes in an array of shapes and finishes, and generally can be used interchangeably on right-hand and left-hand doors. (Be aware, however, that right-hand and left-hand hinges are sometimes different.)

Catches and latches, too, run the gamut in form and style. But style is not a factor with some of the catches cabinetmakers use most, since they are not visible when doors are closed. A number of popular catches have spring clips that hold the door in place until it is pulled open. Others have small magnets that adhere to steel plates. Magnet catches have an advantage in that they work even if a door sags, so long as some part of the magnet comes in contact with the plate.

It is wise to purchase cabinet hardware, even the simple items, after you have settled on the design of the cabinet you plan to build but before you start work on it. That way you avoid the delay and disappointment of almost completing your project and then learning that the hardware you wanted is out of stock or must be specially ordered.

A harmonious medley of hardware. The knobs, hinges and drawer pulls at right are typical of the assortment of cabinet hardware available. The first vertical row contains two H hinges, a butterfly hinge and an oriental snake hinge. In the two middle rows are eight carved wood knobs above four stainless-steel ones. The last row consists of drawer bail pulls in a variety of styles, from modern to traditional Chippendale design.

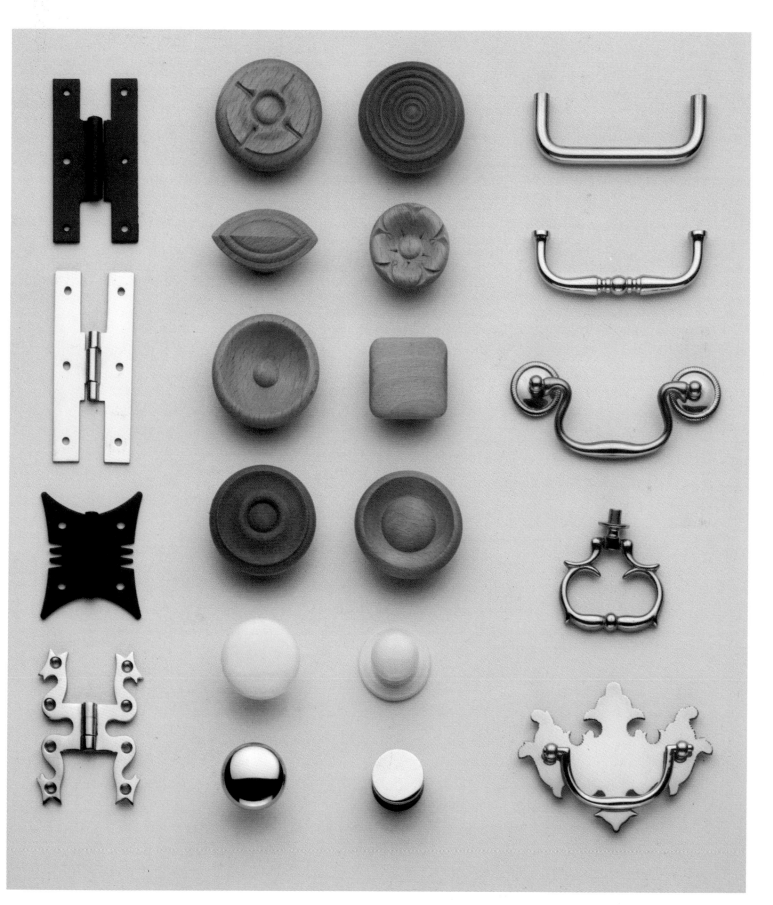

A window seat with storage galore

Having a cozy window seat for observing the world outside makes any room a more interesting place to be. The bedroom window seat below is large enough to stretch out on, and the front is a latched door that opens at the touch to swing down on a piano hinge and reveal the seat as a capacious cabinet. Shelves inside keep a wardrobe of shoes and boots organized out of sight; with the shelves removed, the cabinet accommodates larger objects such as overnight bags.

Sleek-looking and stylish, the cabinet basically is an elongated box. Except for its back, all of its structural components are cut from two 4-by-8-foot sheets of ¾-inch Grade A2 hardwood plywood. Here, birch plywood is used, but plywoods with walnut or cherry surfaces also are prime candidates, especially where the aim is a

natural finish on beautiful wood grain. Whether you cut the plywood pieces or have your lumber dealer do it, make certain that the sheets for your cabinet are a match: The exact thickness of so-called ¾-inch plywood can vary by nearly ⅟₁₆ inch. Plan the cuts ahead of time so that the wood's grain runs parallel to the long dimensions of exterior pieces; the grain will thus blend when the cabinet is done.

Only a few simple tools are called for. In addition to a hammer and screwdriver, you will need a pair of C clamps, a saber saw fitted with a smooth-cutting plywood blade, and a variable-speed drill equipped with both ³⁄₁₆-inch and ³⁄₃₂-inch twist bits as well as a conical countersink bit.

Although not difficult, the traditional cabinetmaking methods used here often call for patience. For example, the entire framework is assembled with counter-

sunk screws *(page 124)* and checked for squareness. The pieces then are taken apart, glue is applied to the joints, and the frame is reassembled with screws. After that, you must let the glue dry for at least 24 hours before continuing.

When you are done, fill in screw holes on the outside of the cabinet with wood putty, and smooth all surfaces with medium (100-grit) and fine (150-grit) sandpaper. Paint the cabinet with enamel undercoat and polyurethane enamel — sanding with very fine (220-grit) sandpaper between coats — or apply a wood stain and finish it with several coats of varnish.

Materials List

Plywood	2 sheets A2-quality ¾" birch plywood, 4' x 8', cut into: 1 bottom piece, 13½" x 76½" 1 door, 13⅜" x 76¼" 1 seat piece, 16" x 78" 2 shelf pieces, 13" x 37¾" 2 endpieces, 15" x 16" 8 shelf supports, 5⅝" x 13" 1 center divider, 12¾" x 13¼" 2 top rails, 3" x 76½" 2 bottom rails, 2½" x 76½" 2 bottom supports, 2½" x 10½" 1 piece A2-quality ¼" birch plywood, 13½" x 76½", for back
Screen molding	¾"-wide pine screen molding, 10' long
Hardware	1 brass piano hinge, 6' long, 1½" wide, with screws 1 push-type latch and door strike
Fasteners	50 No. 8 flat-head wood screws, 1¼" long 4 oz. fourpenny finishing nails 4 oz. steel brads, ¾" long

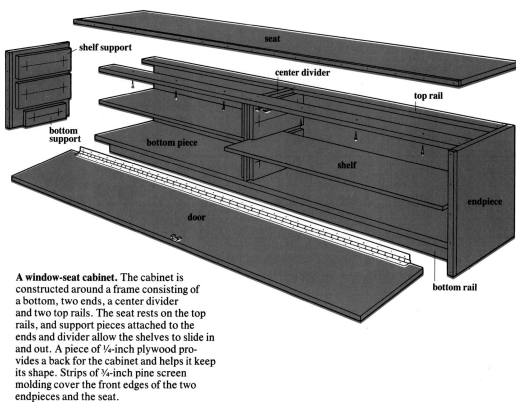

A window-seat cabinet. The cabinet is constructed around a frame consisting of a bottom, two ends, a center divider and two top rails. The seat rests on the top rails, and support pieces attached to the ends and divider allow the shelves to slide in and out. A piece of ¼-inch plywood provides a back for the cabinet and helps it keep its shape. Strips of ¾-inch pine screen molding cover the front edges of the two endpieces and the seat.

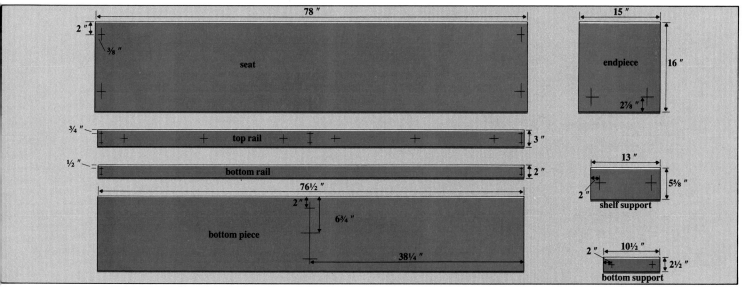

1 **Marking locations for countersunk screw holes.** Using a straightedge and a pencil, draw a line ⅜ inch from each end of the seat and the top-rail and bottom-rail pieces, as shown in the diagram above. Make cross marks on the lines 2 inches from each edge of the seat, ¾ inch from the edges of the two top rails and ½ inch from the edges of the two bottom rails. Draw a line along the lengthwise center of each top rail and make cross marks along the lines at approximately 1-foot intervals; draw a line down the crosswise center of the rails and make cross marks on the lines ¾ inch from each edge. Next, draw a center line perpendicular to the long edge of the bottom piece. Mark the line at the center of the board and 2 inches from each edge. Draw a line 2⅞ inches from one short

edge on each endpiece, and mark the lines 2 inches from each end. Draw a line along the lengthwise center of the eight shelf supports and make cross marks on the lines 2 inches from each end. Finally, draw similar center lines on the two bottom support pieces and make cross marks 2 inches from the ends of each line. ▶

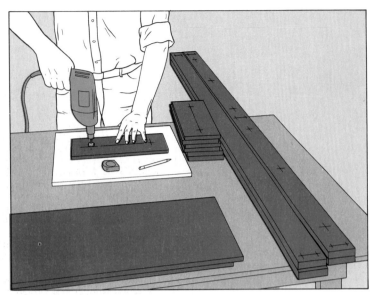

2 **Drilling countersunk screw holes.** Using a drill fitted with a ³/₁₆-inch twist bit, drill screw holes all the way through each of the marked locations — on the seat, bottom, top rails, bottom rails, endpieces, shelf supports and bottom supports. Then use a conical countersink bit to enlarge the openings of the holes on the Grade A side of the shelf supports and bottom supports so that the screwheads will sit flush with the surface of the wood. Finally, use the bit to countersink, from the Grade A side, the holes in the two endpieces, the top and bottom rails and the seat so that the screwheads will sit slightly below the wood's surface. Set the seat and bottom pieces and the four rails aside.

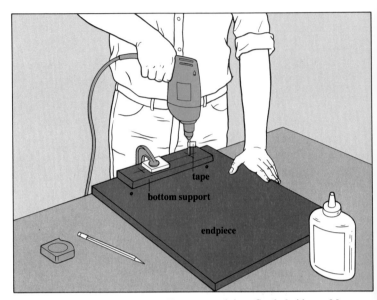

3 **Attaching bottom supports.** Turn one endpiece Grade 2 side up. Measure 2¾ inches from the right edge along its 15-inch side, and mark the spot. Position one end of a bottom support on the mark, aligning the bottom edges of the two pieces. Clamp the two pieces together, inserting a wood scrap to protect the wood. Fit a drill with a ³/₃₂-inch twist bit and wrap tape around the bit 1¼ inches from the tip to gauge the depth of the hole. Drill pilot holes into the endpiece through the holes in the bottom support. Then position one end of the second bottom support 2¾ inches from the left edge of the second endpiece; clamp the pieces and drill pilot holes similarly. Apply glue to the inside of both supports and attach them to the endpieces with 1¼-inch No. 8 wood screws.

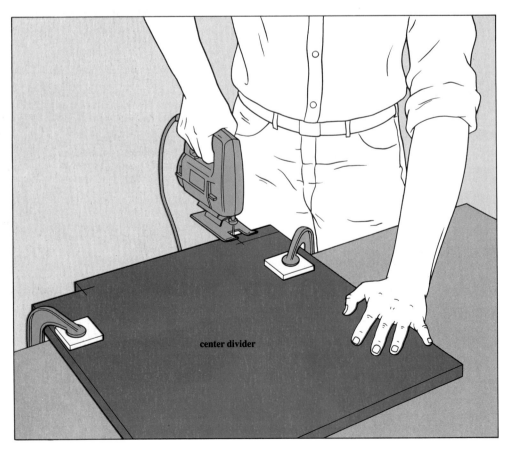

5 **Notching the center divider.** Using a carpenter's square, draw a line ¾ inch from one 13¼-inch edge of the center divider. Make marks 3 inches from each end, and outline notches with the square by drawing perpendicular lines from the marks to the board's edge. Clamp the board to the work surface so the two notch outlines overhang the edge, and cut out the notches using a saber saw fitted with a smooth-cutting plywood blade. The two 3-inch-wide top rails will fit into the notches at what is now the top of the divider.

4 **Attaching shelf supports.** Position what will be the lower shelf support ¼ inch from the 16-inch edge of an endpiece and ¾ inch from the bottom support, using a scrap of ¾-inch plywood on edge as a spacer. Clamp the pieces together, then drill pilot holes in the endpiece through the holes in the support. Position the upper shelf support ¾ inch from the lower one, and drill pilot holes through it into the endpiece similarly. Apply glue to the inner surfaces of both shelf supports and attach them to the endpiece with 1¼-inch No. 8 wood screws. Finally, attach the lower and upper shelf supports to the other endpiece the same way.

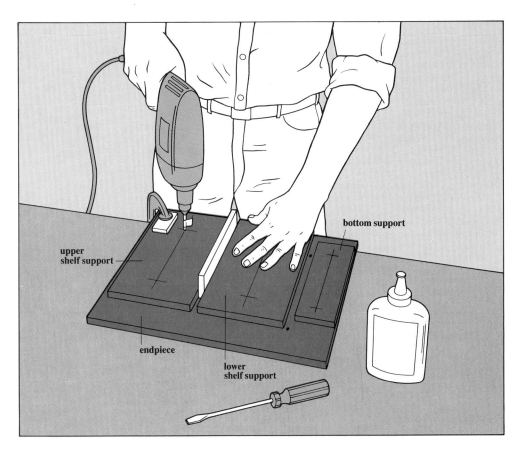

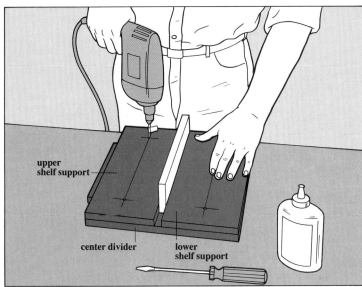

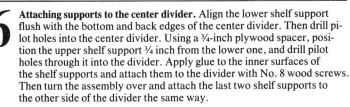

6 **Attaching supports to the center divider.** Align the lower shelf support flush with the bottom and back edges of the center divider. Then drill pilot holes into the center divider. Using a ¾-inch plywood spacer, position the upper shelf support ¾ inch from the lower one, and drill pilot holes through it into the divider. Apply glue to the inner surfaces of the shelf supports and attach them to the divider with No. 8 wood screws. Then turn the assembly over and attach the last two shelf supports to the other side of the divider the same way.

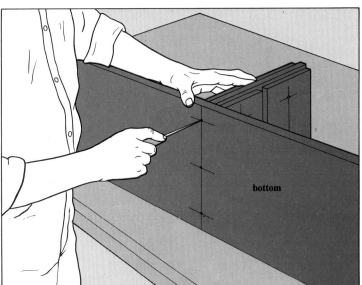

7 **Joining the center divider and bottom.** Stand the center divider and the bottom piece on edge on top of the work surface, as shown above, aligning the center of the divider with the screw holes in the bottom piece. Push an awl through the holes in the bottom to punch marks into the edge of the divider; mark the punched locations with a pencil. Then use a ³⁄₃₂-inch twist bit to drill pilot holes at the marked locations. Finally, attach the bottom piece to the divider with 1¼-inch No. 8 wood screws. ▶

8 **Attaching endpieces to the bottom.** Set the bottom of the cabinet on the work surface with both its ends overhanging. Fit one end of the bottom into the slot between the lower shelf support and the bottom support on one endpiece, aligning the back edges of the bottom and the shelf support. Use a 3/32-inch twist bit to make pilot holes in the edge of the bottom through the holes in the endpiece; attach the endpiece to the bottom with No. 8 wood screws. Fit the bottom onto the endpiece at the other end of the cabinet, drill holes through the endpiece into the bottom (*above*) and attach the two pieces with screws.

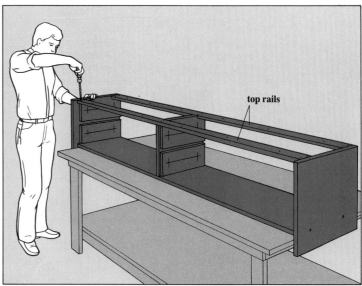

9 **Attaching top rails.** Position one top rail in the rear notch of the divider so that the divider lies directly under the middle pair of holes in the rail. Drill pilot holes into the divider through the rail holes; insert a No. 8 wood screw in one of the holes. Align the rail's back edge with the back edges of the upper shelf supports on the endpieces; drill pilot holes into the supports through the rail holes and fasten the pieces with screws. Fit the other top rail in the divider's front notch and fasten it with one screw. Then measure the distance between the two rails along the top of the divider; attach the front rail to the shelf supports at the same distance from the back rail at both ends. Disassemble the frame; apply glue to all of the joints in Steps 7-9 and reassemble the frame with No. 8 wood screws.

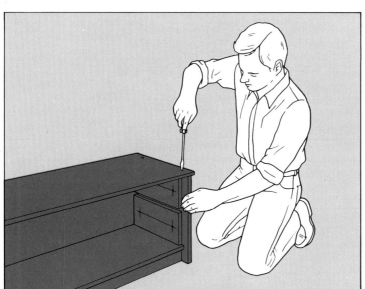

12 **Attaching the seat.** Set the cabinet frame upright on the floor. Place the seat piece on top of it, aligning the back and sides with the back and sides of the frame. Drill 3/32-inch pilot holes into the edges of the endpieces and secure the joints with No. 8 wood screws (*above*). Turn the assembly on its back and drill pilot holes into the lower surface of the seat through the holes in the front top rail. Finally, disassemble the pieces, apply glue to the joint surfaces and reassemble the cabinet with screws.

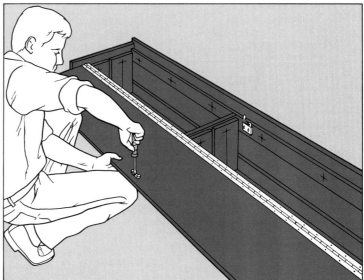

13 **Attaching the door.** Center a 72-inch piano hinge on the edge of the cabinet bottom. Drill pilot holes into the bottom through the hinge's center and end holes; fasten the hinge with the manufacturer's screws. Drill holes through the remaining holes in the hinge. Draw a line on the door's inner surface 3/4 inch from one long edge. Center the door between the endpieces and align the hinge on the line. Drill pilot holes in the door through the middle and end hinge holes. Secure the hinge with screws. Close the door to check the alignment, then drill holes through the remaining hinge holes and screw the hinge to the door. Following the manufacturer's instructions, attach a push-type latch to the front top rail and a strike to the door.

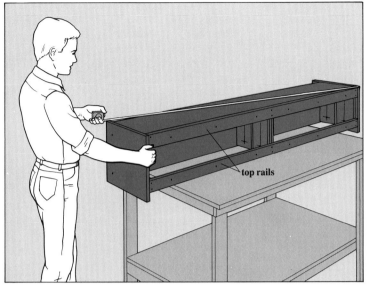

10 **Attaching the back.** Lay the cabinet on its face on top of the work surface. Apply glue to the back edges of the bottom, center divider, shelf supports and rear top rail. Then align the back's top edge with the upper surface of the rear top rail and fasten the two pieces together with fourpenny finishing nails spaced at 1-foot intervals. Next, measure the diagonals between opposite corners of the cabinet with a tape measure to check that the frame is square; the two distances should be equal. Adjust the frame by pushing the corners of the longer diagonal toward each other. Finally, nail the back to the bottom and the shelf supports with fourpenny finishing nails 1 foot apart. Let the glued pieces dry for 24 hours.

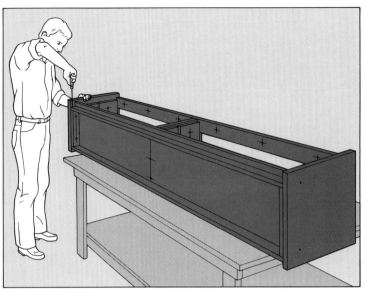

11 **Attaching the bottom rails.** Align the first bottom rail against the back edge of the bottom support on each endpiece so that the top edge of the rail abuts the bottom of the cabinet. Drill pilot holes into the edges of the bottom supports through the holes in the rail. Apply glue to the edges of the bottom supports and attach the rail to them with No. 8 wood screws. Then turn the cabinet on its back and attach the front bottom rail to the front edges of the bottom supports with glue and screws the same way *(above)*.

14 **Attaching edge molding.** With the cabinet still on its back, apply glue to one edge of the seat piece at a time and lay a strip of pine screen molding on top of it, aligning the molding with the upper and lower surfaces of the seat. Then fasten the molding with ¾-inch-long steel brads. Finally, fasten molding strips to the edges of the two endpieces with glue and ¾-inch brads the same way.

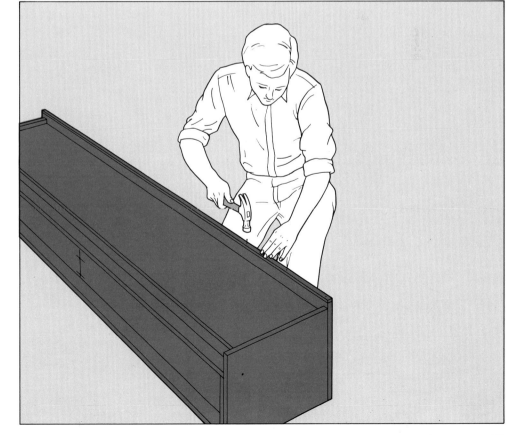

A classic country cupboard

In the 19th Century, traveling joiners and cabinetmakers produced much of the furniture for America's rural households, creating tables, chairs and chests that are still prized for their craftsmanship. Cupboards like the one below were among the period's most popular pieces; their covered shelves served many purposes, providing storage in various rooms of the house. Originally made with hand tools and local woods, these country classics are easily re-created using modern methods and materials — at a fraction of what an antique would cost.

The cupboard is basically a box whose legs are an integral part of its structure. The top, sides and bottom are made of 18-inch-wide panels of pine boards glued together by the manufacturer. The preglued panels, available only in pine, are sold at most home-improvement stores; the other parts are cut from dimension lumber and plywood sheets, both easily found at lumberyards. Have the dealer saw the pieces to the sizes specified in the Materials List, or cut them yourself. Then label all the pieces for reference.

In order to build the cupboard, you will need a hammer and screwdriver, several C clamps and corner clamps, and a variable-speed power drill with $3/32$-inch and $3/16$-inch twist bits and a $3/8$-inch spade bit. The project also requires cutting grooves called dadoes and rabbets in the surface of wood so that pieces can be fitted together in snug joints. As shown in the exploded diagram at right, a dado is a rectangular groove cut at right angles to the edge grain of a board; a rabbet is an L-shaped groove cut along the edge or end of a board. Cutting the grooves goes quickly with a router *(page 122)*, a power tool that can be rented; you will have to buy a $1/2$-inch dado bit to use with it.

To make sure the pieces of the structural frame — the carcass, as cabinetmakers call it — fit together correctly, they are first assembled with screws. Then they are taken apart, glued and screwed together again.

After you have assembled the cupboard, drive all the nails below the surface of the wood with a nail set, and cover screwheads and nailheads with wood putty. Smooth the surfaces with medium (100-grit) sandpaper and seal them with alcohol-thinned shellac mixed at a ratio of four parts alcohol to one part shellac. Finally, sand the surface again with fine (150-grit) sandpaper and finish it with two or three coats of an alkyd enamel paint, sanding between coats with very fine (220-grit) sandpaper.

Materials List

Pine panels	6 panels preglued 1 " pine, 18 " x 48 ", cut into: 1 top panel, 39 " x 17 " 2 side panels, 37½ " x 15¼ " 1 bottom piece, 36 " x 15 " 2 adjustable shelves, 35⅜ " x 14¾ "
1 x 4	6 ' clear pine 1 x 4, cut into: 2 top supports, 36 " long
1 x 3	16 ' clear pine 1 x 3, cut into: 2 side stiles, 37½ " long 1 face-frame backing strip, at least 36 " long 2 rails, at least 34 " long
1 x 2	6 ' clear pine 1 x 2, cut into: 1 face-frame backing strip, at least 36 " long 1 center stile, at least 32 " long
Plywood	1 sheet 4 ' x 4 ' AA-quality ¼ " plywood, cut into: 1 back panel, 36 " x 31¼ "

	1 sheet 4 ' x 4 ' AA-quality ½ " birch plywood, cut to measure into 2 door panels, about 28 " x 15 "
Lath	16 ' clear pine ¼ " x 1¾ " lath
Molding	8 ' roman ogee cap molding ¾ " x ½ " molding stock, 1 ' long
Hardware	2 pairs 3 " H hinges, with screws 8 metal bracket pins 2 knobs, with screws
Nails	1 lb. fourpenny finishing nails 2 oz. ½ " brads 4 oz. paneling nails, 1 " long
Screws	20 No. 8 flat-head wood screws, 1¼ " long 2 No. 6 oval-head brass-plated wood screws, 1 " long
For the jig	1 clear pine 1 x 3, 27 " long

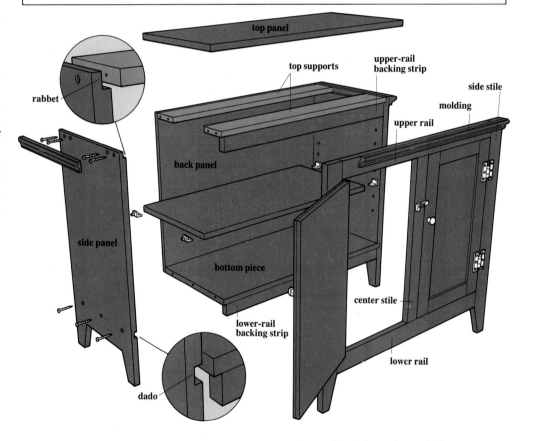

A country cupboard. The structural frame of the cupboard is formed by the bottom piece, the two side panels and the two top supports. The ends of the bottom piece are held in dadoes cut into the base of the sides, and the top supports and back panel fit into rabbets cut along the top and rear edges of the sides. But those are the only joints in the cupboard that require preparatory cutting.

The stiles (vertical elements) and rails (horizontal pieces) that make up the face frame on the front of the cabinet are not joined to one another at all; they are nailed and glued to other parts of the cupboard behind them. And the doors, which look like panel construction requiring mortise-and-tenon joints, are actually assemblies of plywood and lath. The cupboard has two adjustable shelves, only one of which is shown here to simplify the drawing.

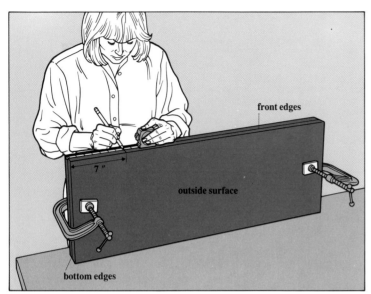

1 **Marking dado and rabbet locations.** Inserting scraps to protect the wood, clamp the two side panels together so that the edges are flush and the better sides face outward. Label the front, back and bottom edges and the two outside surfaces for reference. With the assembly on its back edge, measure and mark the front edges 7 inches from the bottom edges; make a second mark that is closer to the bottom by a distance equal to the exact thickness of the cabinet's bottom piece. (This piece should be ¾ inch thick; measure it to be certain.) Then measure the thickness of the top supports — they, too, should be ¾ inch thick — and mark this distance from the top onto the front edges. Turn the assembly over, and mark the same distances on the back edges of the panels.

2 **Drawing cutting lines for the router.** Unclamp the panels and extend the marks from the front and back edges onto the inside surfaces. Lay the panels inner surfaces up, front edge to front edge, and align the ends. Use a straightedge to connect the marks with lines drawn across the panels. Finally, draw a line ¼ inch from the back edge of each panel (above).

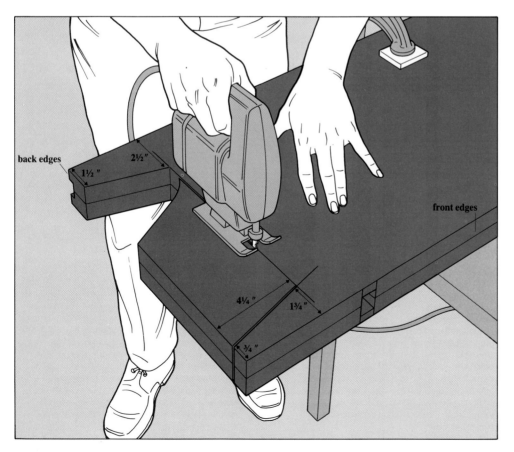

4 **Cutting the legs.** Align the side panels, inner surface to inner surface, and clamp them together to the worktable so that their bottom edges extend at least 6 inches beyond the table's edge. Using a straightedge, draw a line 4¼ inches from the bottom edges of the panels. Mark the line 1¾ inches from the front edges of the panels and 2½ inches from the back edges.

Along the bottom of the top panel, make marks ¾ inch from the front edge and 1½ inches from the back. Draw straight lines connecting these marks with the marks on the 4¼-inch line, as seen at left. Use a saber saw (page 120) to cut out the inner section outlined in pencil, leaving angled legs at the bottom of each side panel. Cut along the two angled lines first, then make a curved cut from the bottom edge to the intersection of the horizontal and angled lines on one side. Finally, cut along the horizontal line to the other angled cut (left).

3 **Cutting dadoes and rabbets.** Measure from the outside edge of the router's base plate to the nearest edge of the cutting bit *(inset).* Mark this distance at several points to the outside of each dado cutting line, and align and clamp a straight, 3-foot-long 1-by-3 along each set of marks. The boards will guide the router so that the bit cuts a channel inside the cutting lines.

Wearing goggles, stand at the bottom end of the panels. Start the router and move it left to right across the panels, guiding it against the far 1-by-3. Then move the router in a right-to-left pass against the near 1-by-3.

Next, clamp a 1-by-3 parallel to the rabbet cutting line at the top of the panels and as far from that line as the distance between the base plate and the near edge of the bit. Guiding the router against the 1-by-3, make a pass from right to left along the cutting line; shift the board ⅜ inch closer to the top of the panels and make a second pass from left to right in order to cut a ¾-inch rabbet. Finally, use the router and another guide strip to cut a ¼-inch-wide rabbet along each panel's back edge in a single pass.

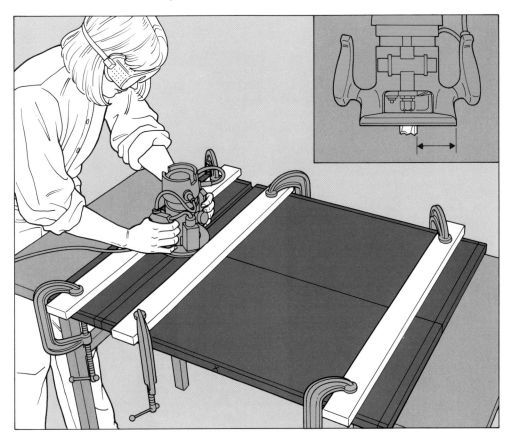

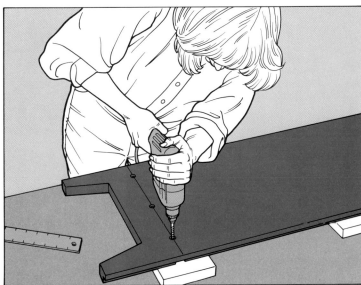

5 **Drilling holes for countersunk screws.** Unclamp the panels and lay one of them, dadoed side down, on a scrap of wood on the work surface. Using a straightedge, draw a line 6⅝ inches from the bottom of the panel; the line should exactly bisect the width of the dado. Mark the line at its midpoint and 2 inches from each end. Then draw a line ⅜ inch from the top of the panel so that it bisects the ¾-inch-wide rabbet. Mark this line 1 inch and 1½ inches from each end. Using a ⅜-inch spade bit with tape wrapped around it ⅛ inch from its tip, drill ⅛-inch-deep counterbore holes at each mark. Then use a ³⁄₁₆-inch twist bit to drill shank holes all the way through each of the marked locations *(above).* Mark and drill screw holes in the other side panel the same way.

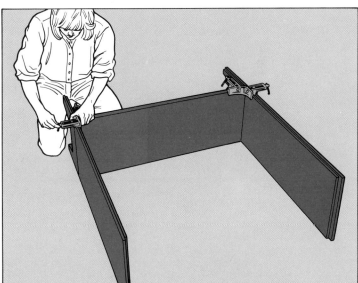

6 **Attaching side panels to the bottom piece.** Set a side panel on its front edge on the floor. Insert one end of the bottom piece all the way into the dado on the panel, making sure the front edge of the bottom piece is flush with the front edge of the panel; secure the two pieces together with a corner clamp. Then fit and clamp together the other side panel and the other end of the bottom piece. Now turn the assembly upright on its legs and inspect the two joints; adjust the alignment if necessary by loosening the clamps slightly and moving the pieces until all the front edges are flush. Then retighten the clamps. ▶

7 **Attaching the top supports.** Position the ends of one top support in the rabbets on top of the side panels so that the support's front edge is flush with the front edges of the sides. Clamp the support to the panels with corner clamps.

Drill through the holes in the side panels with a 3/32-inch twist bit to make 1-inch-deep pilot holes in the ends of the bottom piece and the front top support. Then secure the joints with 1¼-inch-long No. 8 wood screws. Fit the ends of the other top support in the rabbets so that its back edge is flush with the inside surface of the rabbets on the back edges of the side panels. Then drill pilot holes into the support's ends (*right*) and attach the sides to it with screws.

Now check the alignment of the assembly by turning the cabinet face down on the floor and fitting the ¼-inch-thick plywood back panel into the rabbets along the rear edges of the side panels. The pieces are correctly aligned if the back panel fits snugly into the rabbets. Remove the back panel and the corner clamps.

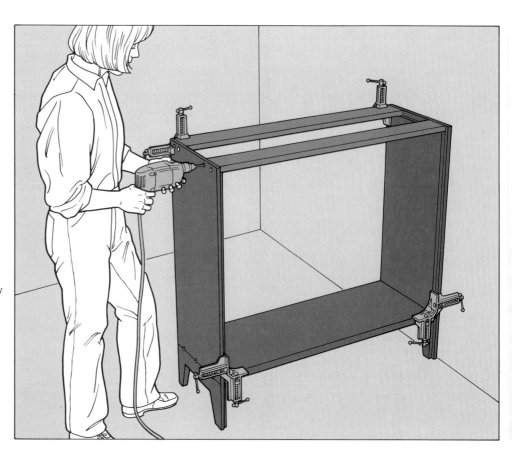

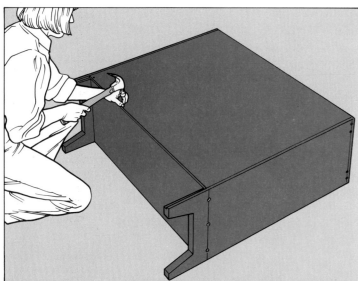

9 **Attaching the back panel.** Lay the cabinet face down on the floor. Apply a bead of glue to the back edges of the bottom piece and the rear top support and to the rabbets on the back edges of the side panels. Fit the back panel into the rabbets, flush with the upper surface of the top support and the underside of the bottom piece. Fasten the back panel to the bottom piece with five 1-inch-long paneling nails, 9 inches apart. Start nails into the back panel on the remaining three sides, but do not drive them in yet. Measure the diagonal distances across the back of the cabinet between opposite corners. The measurements should be equal; if not, push the corners of the longer diagonal toward each other until the two distances match. Then drive in all the nails.

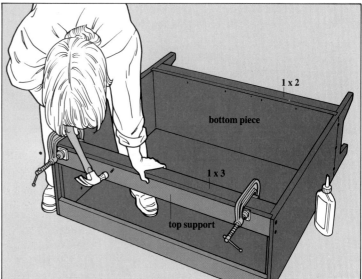

10 **Attaching the rail backing strips.** Now turn the cabinet over onto its back. Measure the exact distances between the inside surfaces of the side panels at the top and bottom of the front of the cabinet (they should be about 35¾ inches). Then — using a backsaw and a miter box to achieve perfectly squared ends — cut a length of 1-by-2 and a length of 1-by-3 to fit the opening between the panels. Apply glue to one long edge of the 1-by-2, then clamp it to the underside of the bottom piece so that it is flush with the front edges of the side panels, and nail it in place with four fourpenny finishing nails driven through the bottom piece. Glue, clamp and nail the 1-by-3 to the underside of the top support similarly (*above*).

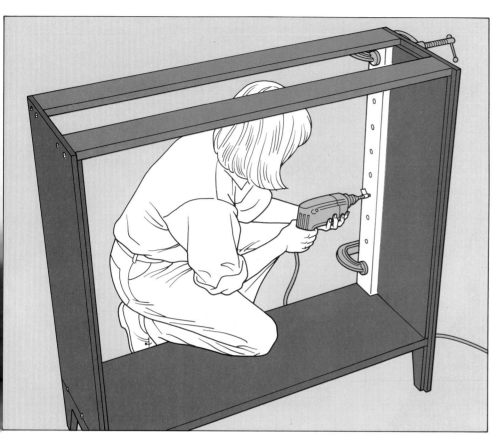

8 **Drilling shelf-bracket holes.** Make a drilling jig out of a 27-inch-long 1-by-3 *(page 31, Step 7)*. Set the jig upright against one side panel inside the cabinet so that its edge is flush with the front edge of the panel, as shown at left. Clamp the jig to the panel, tape the bit 1¼ inches from the tip (to allow ¾ inch for the thickness of the jig plus ½ inch for the depth of the hole) and drill ½-inch-deep bracket holes into the panel through the holes in the jig.

Unclamp the pieces, align the edge of the jig flush with the inside surface of the rabbet along the rear edge of the panel and drill holes there. Next, drill front and rear bracket holes in the other side panel. Then label all the pieces, disassemble them, apply glue and reassemble each joint in turn, fixing the joints with screws.

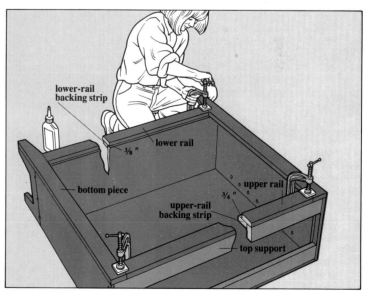

11 **Attaching side stiles.** Along one long edge, make a mark 4 inches from the end of a 37½-inch 1-by-3. Mark the end of the board 1 inch from the marked edge. Use a straightedge to connect the marks, then cut along the line with a saber saw to make an angled leg; mark and cut an angled leg on the other 37½-inch 1-by-3 side stile. With the cabinet still on its back, apply glue along the front edges of the side panels and on the endmost 1½ inches of both rail backing strips. Position a side stile on the front edge of each side panel, the straight edge of the stile flush with the panel's outer surface. Nail the stiles to the panels with five fourpenny finishing nails spaced 2 inches from each end and at 8-inch intervals between.

12 **Attaching the rails.** Measure the distance between the inside edges of the stiles, and cut two 1-by-3 rails to that length. Apply glue to the front edge of the top support and the adjacent 2 inches of the upper-rail backing strip. Nail the upper rail to the backing strip, its upper edge flush with the upper surface of the top support, leaving the lower ¾ inch of the rail backing strip exposed *(above, near cutaway)*. Then glue and nail the lower 1-by-3 rail to its backing strip and the edge of the bottom piece so that the top of the rail is ⅜ inch below the bottom piece's upper surface *(above, far cutaway)*. Tighten C clamps onto each inner corner as seen above, putting scraps under the clamp jaws to protect the wood. ▶

13

Attaching the divider. Measure the distance between the inside edges of the upper and lower rails at their midpoints, then cut a 1-by-2 center stile to that length. Mark the midpoints of the rails and the centers of the ends of the 1-by-2 stile; apply glue to the upper ¾ inch and the lower ⅜ inch of the back of the center stile, then fit the stile between the rails so the marks line up. Clamp the stile's top to the face-frame backing strip and nail its bottom end to the edge of the bottom piece with a fourpenny finishing nail *(right)*.

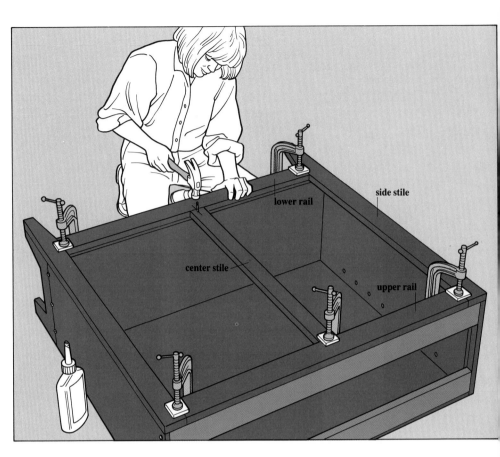

16

Making the doors. Measure the height and width of each door opening — in this case, about 28 by 15 inches — then cut a rectangle of ½-inch plywood ⅛ inch smaller in each dimension. Next, cut two pieces of lath the same length as one door panel. Apply glue to one side of the laths, and position them along the two long edges of the panel, as shown above. Nail the laths in place with ½-inch-long brads spaced at 8-inch intervals. Now measure the distance between the inside edges of the lath strips, and cut two strips to that length. Attach those strips along the top and bottom edges of the panel with glue and brads. Now cut and attach lath strips to frame the edges of the other door panel the same way.

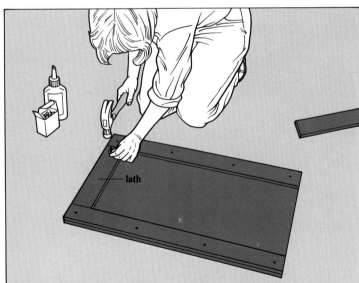

17

Attaching door knobs and latches. Mark the center of each inside vertical lath strip 18 inches from the bottom. Drill ³⁄₃₂-inch holes through lath and door panel at the marks. Attach a wood knob to each door with the screws provided by the knob manufacturer. Now cut two 1½-inch pieces of ¾-by-½-inch molding stock. Bevel one wide edge of each piece with coarse (60-grit) sandpaper. Then drill a ³⁄₁₆-inch hole through each piece ⅜ inch from the beveled edge, as seen in the inset. Make marks 22 inches from the bottom and ⅜ inch from each side edge of the center stile. Drill ¹⁄₁₆-inch-diameter pilot holes ½ inch deep at the marks and attach the pieces to the stile with 1-inch-long No. 6 oval-head brass wood screws.

90

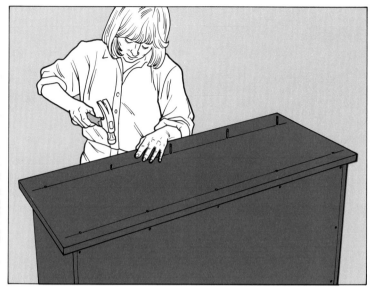

14 **Attaching the top.** Now set the cabinet upright on the floor. Draw parallel lines on the top piece 1 inch from the back and 2 inches from the front, and position the top so that it is flush with the back edges of the side panels and overhangs those panels by an equal amount on both sides. Apply glue to the top edges of the cabinet's back and sides and to the upper surfaces of the top supports, then nail the top in place: Use fourpenny finishing nails driven at 8-inch intervals into the top supports along the lines.

15 **Attaching molding.** Use a miter box to cut one end of a 40-inch strip of roman ogee cap molding at a 45° angle *(page 31, Step 8).* Align the inside of the mitered cut with one side of the cabinet; mark the molding where it crosses the other side *(above).* Put the strip back in the miter box and cut toward the mark to miter that end. Apply glue to the back of the molding and nail it in place with three fourpenny finishing nails. Now miter one end of an 18-inch molding strip. Butt the mitered end against a mitered end of the front molding, and mark the strip where it crosses the back of the cabinet. Make a straight cut at the mark, then glue and nail the molding in place. Cut and attach a molding strip for the cabinet's other side.

18 **Attaching the doors.** Lay the cabinet on its back and position one of the doors in its opening. Insert small pieces of cardboard into the space around the door to center it in the frame.

Position an H hinge 3 inches from the top of the door so that the knuckle of the hinge is directly above the space between the door and the frame. Mark screw-hole locations on the door and frame through the holes in the leaves of the hinge. Align another H hinge 3 inches from the bottom of the door, and mark the screw-hole locations there.

Tape a 1/8-inch twist bit 5/8 inch from its tip and use it to drill 5/8-inch-deep pilot holes at all the marked locations. Then attach the door to the cabinet by its hinges, using the screws supplied with the hinge. Fit the other door inside its opening, and attach it to the cabinet with H hinges the same way.

Modules for a wall system

The ever-growing desire for family information and entertainment systems has presented homemakers and decorators with an interesting problem in spatial relations: how to find enough shelf and cabinet space to hold all the stereos, televisions, VCRs and computers, along with the usual collections of books and bric-a-brac. The modular wall system shown here answers this need with panache: It integrates general-use and special-purpose storage in a wall-hugging expanse of fine wood furniture, which can be built for a fraction of the cost of ready-mades.

In this system, two basic components — a cabinet below and a bookcase above *(pages 94-102)* — are the modules on which all of the other components are patterned. Their simple design may be repeated again and again, their dimensions varied or details changed, but the result will always look sleek and well-balanced.

Because you build it yourself, you can scale the system to fit your own particular wall. Or you can create a basic grouping and expand or modify it to keep pace with your family's changing needs. Removable screws connect the components to each other, making the system easy to augment or rearrange.

Illustrated here from left to right are, first, a basic bookcase in its traditional role atop a basic cabinet, which in this case contains a television set resting on a pull-out pedestal *(pages 104-106)* that rotates for comfortable viewing. Beside them, two narrow cases and cabinets create an audio center *(pages 107-111),* which provides a custom fit for standard stereo components while leaving plenty of space for records and tapes. Next, a desk *(pages 112-117)* features a slide-out shelf to enlarge its working surface or support a computer keyboard. The small bookcase suspended above it *(pages 118-119)* keeps manuals and other reference works within reach. Finally, a cabinet bears a lighted case *(page 103)* outfitted with glass shelves to show off a prized collection — here, gemstones.

Two basic units

Building blocks for the modular wall system on pages 92-93, the cabinet base and bookcase top at right display a simplicity of design that invites repetition. The construction methods make it easy to modify the dimensions of the units and adjust their details to suit your special needs.

The cabinet shown is 32 inches wide, 32 inches tall and 20¾ inches deep; the bookcase is also 32 inches wide, but 47½ inches tall and 12¼ inches deep. Both are built of birch plywood with facings, shelf edgings, top edgings and internal supports of clear lumber. Pine is specified in the Materials List, but fir, spruce or another softwood can be substituted.

Strong, uniform and warp-resistant, birch plywood offers a smooth surface for a painted finish. If you prefer an oil or varnish finish, buy a more decorative plywood, such as oak, walnut or cherry. Use matching hardwood for facings and edgings; conceal other visible plywood edges with wood-veneer tape and fill screw holes with matching wood plugs.

Made in the dimensions here, the case, shelves and doors of each unit can be cut from a 4-by-8-foot sheet of plywood. Plan a cutting pattern on graph paper, allowing at least ³⁄₁₆ inch between parts for each kerf, or saw cut. Position each component lengthwise on the paper so that when you take your pattern to the lumberyard to have the plywood cut, the grain will run lengthwise in every piece.

You can cut the plywood yourself with a power saw *(pages 121-123)*. A backsaw and miter box will do for the rest of the wood. Before or after cutting, label each piece in pencil for reference.

A power drill makes quick work of the counterbored holes for screws, and a saber saw is ideal for cutting out mortises for hinges. The rabbet joints between the back and side panels require a router and rabbeting bit; the router can be rented. You will also need an assortment of basic hand tools — hammer, carpenter's square, screwdriver, nail set, C clamps, steel measuring tape and straightedge.

Once the units are built, set nails, and fill dents and screw holes with spackle. Work spackle into the raw edges of doors and shelves. Sand with medium (100-grit), then fine (150-grit) paper, apply a sealer, and finish with oil-based enamel.

Instructions for the cabinet begin opposite, and for the bookcase on page 100.

Building the Cabinet

A sturdy storage cabinet. Birch plywood makes up the body of this basic cabinet, and a frame of 1-by-2s and 1-by-3s forms a smooth front facing. Rabbet joints along the back edges and countersunk screws ensure a tight construction. The plywood doors swing easily on semiconcealed hinges recessed into mortises in the door edges; magnetic catches hold the doors closed.

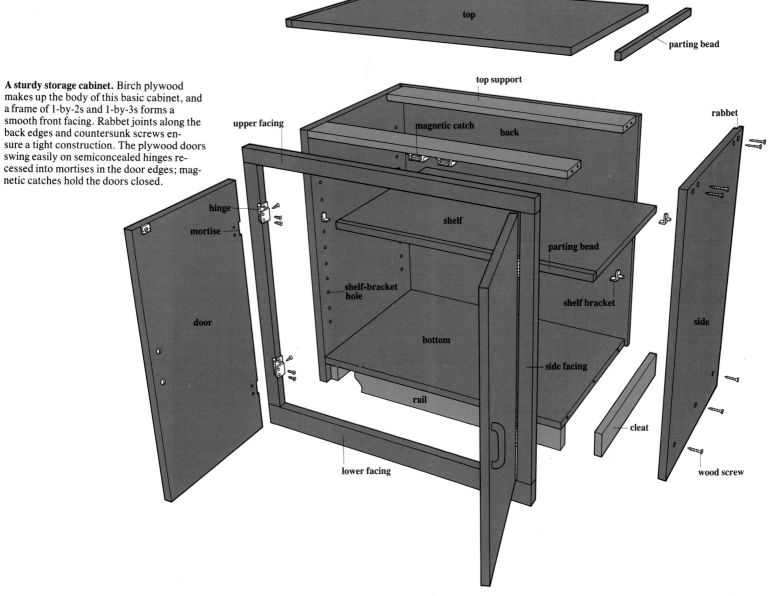

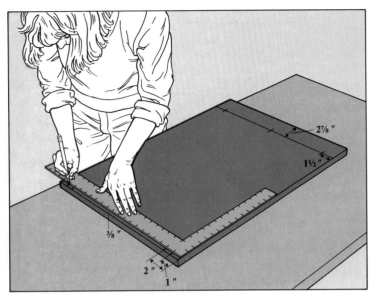

1 **Marking screw-hole positions on side panels.** Lay a side panel, better face upward, on a worktable. Using a carpenter's square, draw a line 2⅞ inches from what will be the bottom edge. Mark for screw holes on the line 1½ inches from each end and in the center. Draw a second line ⅜ inch from the top edge and mark it 1 inch and 2 inches from each end for two pairs of holes. Place the panel on scrap wood. Using a ⅜-inch spade bit and a 3/16-inch twist bit, drill counterbored screw holes as described in Step 5, page 87. Mark and drill the second side panel the same way.

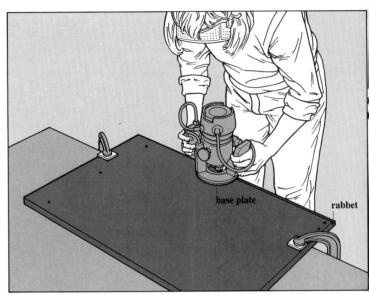

2 **Cutting a rabbet.** Turn one side panel over, better surface down. Inserting scraps to protect the wood, clamp it to the worktable with what will be the panel's back edge overhanging the table by several inches. Fit a router with a ⅜-inch rabbeting bit *(page 122)*, set ⅜ inch below the base plate. Wearing goggles, start the router. Rest the base plate at the left-hand corner of the panel. Push the router into the panel until the bit guide hits the edge, then move the router from left to right to cut the rabbet *(above)*. Cut a rabbet in the back edge of the other side panel in the same way.

5 **Attaching the rear top support.** Stand the cabinet on one side. Align the ends of the rear top support with the top edges of the side panels and the inner edges of the rabbets. Using a 3/32-inch bit, drill through the screw holes into the end of the top support *(right)* and drive the screws. Carefully turn the cabinet over and attach the other end. Make a drilling jig out of a 27-inch-long 1-by-3 *(page 31, Step 7)*, then follow the techniques described on page 89, Step 8, to drill shelf-bracket holes and to disassemble, glue and reassemble the cabinet. Install the back panel as on page 88, Step 9.

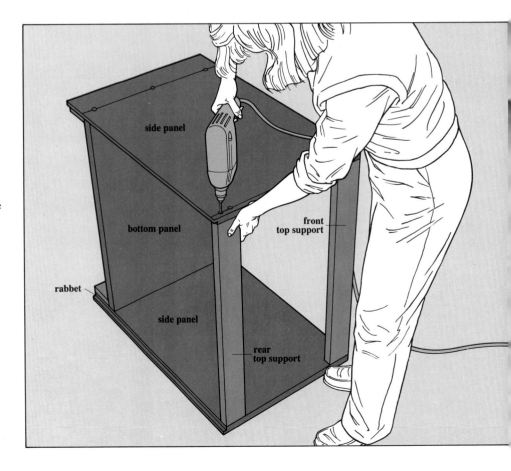

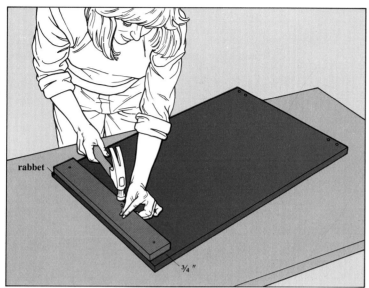

3 **Attaching a cleat.** Spread glue on the back of the panel between the bottom edge and the lower screw holes. Align a 1-by-3 cleat with the bottom of the panel and the inner edge of the rabbet, leaving a ¾-inch space at the front of the panel. Nail the cleat in place with four 1¼-inch brads, evenly spaced. Attach the other cleat to the other side panel.

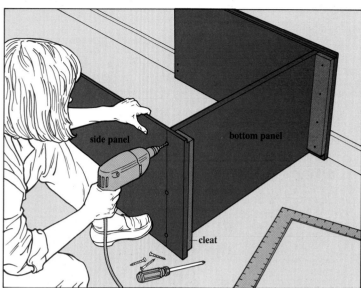

4 **Joining the side panels to the bottom panel.** Set the bottom panel on the floor, long edge up, one end braced against a wall. Set a side panel, rabbeted edge up, perpendicular to the bottom panel, aligning the screw holes with the end of the bottom panel. Check the angle with a carpenter's square, then drill through one hole into the bottom panel using a ³⁄₃₂-inch twist bit; drive in a 1½-inch No. 8 flat-head screw. Recheck the angle, drill the remaining holes and drive the screws. Turn the assembly so the side panel is against the wall, and attach the other side panel the same way (above). Place a top support, edge up, on the floor between the side panels, aligning its ends with the panel corners. Drill through the holes into each end of the top support, and drive the screws.

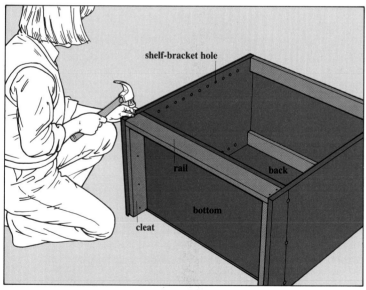

6 **Nailing the rail.** Lay the cabinet on its back. Apply glue to the front ends of the cleats and to the top edge of the 1-by-3 rail piece. Set the rail on the cleats with its top edge against the bottom panel. Drive two fourpenny nails ⅜ inch from each end of the rail into the cleats (above). Set the cabinet upright and nail through the bottom panel into the rail at 8-inch intervals, ⅜ inch from the front edge of the bottom panel.

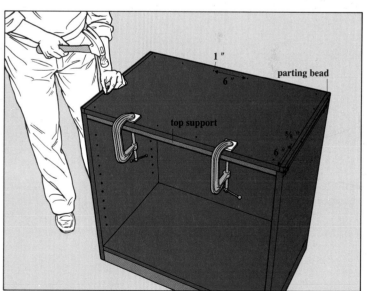

7 **Installing the top.** Attach a 20-inch strip of parting bead to each end of the top with glue and four 1¼-inch brads, evenly spaced. Spread glue on the top supports and the top edges of the sides. Align the top at all the corners, and clamp it to the front top support with C clamps padded with scrap wood. Nail the top in place with 1¼-inch brads 1 inch from the front and back edges, at 6-inch intervals. Then drive two brads at each end, 6 inches from the corners and ⅝ inch from the edge, angled slightly outward (above). Prepare for stacking the bookcase on the cabinet while the glue dries (about one hour): Use a ³⁄₃₂-inch bit to drill four pilot holes through the top for the upper-unit connecting screws, 1½ inches from each end and 3½ inches and 10 inches from the back edge. ▶

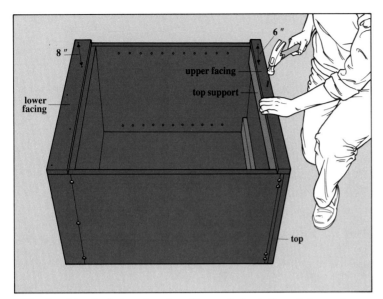

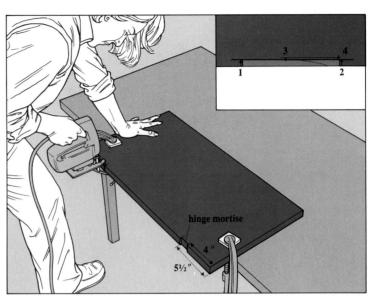

8 **Attaching the facings.** Lay the cabinet on its back. Spread glue on the front rail. Set the 1-by-3 lower facing on the rail so that their bottom edges are aligned and the ends of the facing are flush with the cabinet sides. Nail the facing in place with 1¼-inch brads hammered in 8 inches apart in a staggered row. Apply glue to the front edges of the top and the top support. Align the edge of the 1-by-2 upper facing with the surface of the top and the facing's ends with the cabinet sides. Nail the facing in place with 1¼-inch brads spaced at 6-inch intervals *(above)*. Then measure the space between the upper and lower facing on each side of the cabinet. Cut 1-by-2 side facings to that length and attach them following the technique described on page 30, Step 5.

9 **Cutting hinge mortises.** Clamp a door panel, better side downward, to the worktable so that what will be the hinged edge overhangs the table by about 4 inches. Mark short lines for hinge locations perpendicular to the edge of the panel, 4 inches and 5½ inches from each corner. Connect each pair of lines with a line parallel to the door edge: This line should be as far from the edge as the exact thickness of a hinge leaf. Using a saber saw fitted with a plywood-cutting blade, cut first along the two short lines *(inset, 1 and 2)*, then cut inward in a curve and continue on the long line *(3)*. Finally, cut in the opposite direction on the long line to remove the remaining wood *(4)*. Cut the second hinge mortise similarly, then mark and cut mortises in the second door panel.

11 **Marking hinge positions.** Put a door in place in the cabinet. Insert scraps of cardboard at the door's upper and lower edges to align it evenly and hold it steady. Mark where the top and bottom of each hinge leaf meet the side facing *(right)*, then remove the door. Align the second door and mark its hinge-leaf positions on the opposite side facing.

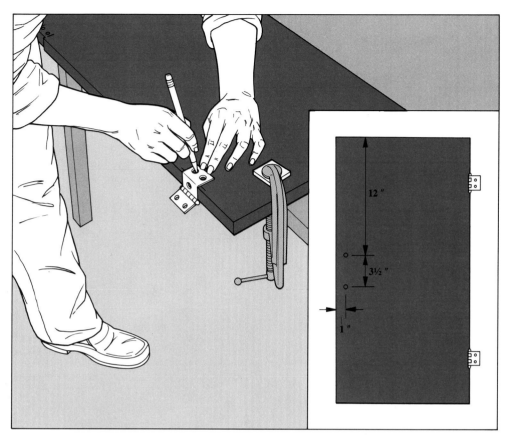

10 **Attaching hinges and handles.** With the door face downward, fit the L-shaped leaf of a hinge in a mortise. Mark screw-hole positions on the door through the hinge holes *(left)*. Using a ¹⁄₁₆-inch bit, drill ½-inch-deep pilot holes at the marks; screw the hinge in place. Attach the second hinge. Turn the door face up-ward. For the handle, mark two screw-hole positions, each 1 inch from the non-hinged edge, one 12 inches from the top edge and the other 3½ inches below that *(inset)*. Put scrap wood beneath the marks and drill holes through the door. Screw the handle in place. Attach the hinges and handle to the second door.

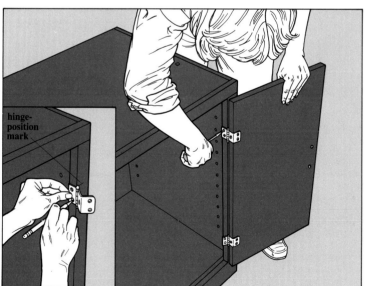

12 **Hanging the doors.** Remove a hinge from one door. Fit the hinge's straight leaf on the inside edge of each side facing between each pair of hinge-position marks and trace the screw holes *(inset)*. With a ¹⁄₁₆-inch bit, drill a ½-inch-deep pilot hole at each mark. Replace the hinge on the door. Align the upper hinge of the door with the corresponding pilot holes, supporting the bottom of the door with your toe *(above)*. Screw the hinge in place, but not tightly. Align the lower hinge with its pilot holes and screw it in place, then tighten both sets of screws. Now hang the other door.

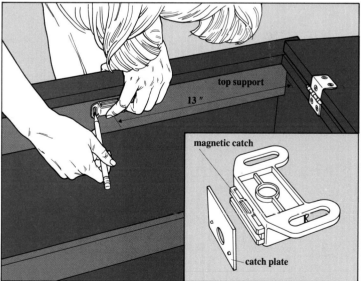

13 **Installing magnetic catches.** Lay the cabinet on its back. Measure along the top support and make a mark 13 inches from one side. Center a catch *(inset)* at the mark, aligning its magnet with the back edge of the upper facing. Trace the screw holes. Set the catch aside. Drill ½-inch-deep pilot holes at the marks. Screw the catch in place snugly, but not tightly. Stick the catch plate to the magnet, bumps outward. Close the door firmly so the bumps leave dents in the door. Screw the plate to the door at the dents. Close the door to check the catch position, then tighten the screws. Now install the other catch and plate. Attach parting bead to the front edge of the shelf *(page 97, Step 7)*, and finish the cabinet.

Building the Bookcase

A versatile bookcase. Designed to sit atop a cabinet, this bookcase is built like an open box fitted with adjustable shelves. The case and shelves are plywood; the case is braced at the corners with 1-by-2 cleats. Facings cut from 1-by-2s trim the front of the case; parting-bead strips protect the front edges of the shelves.

Materials List			
Plywood	1 sheet A2-quality ¾ " birch plywood, cut into: 2 sides, 11½ " x 47½ " 2 ends, 11⅛ " x 30½ " 4 shelves, 10½ " x 30¼ " 1 piece A2-quality ¼ " birch plywood, 31⅛ " x 46 ", for back	**Parting bead**	11 ' parting bead, ½ " x ¾ ", cut into 4 shelf edges, 30¼ " long
		Hardware	12 No. 8 flat-head wood screws, 1½ " long 16-gauge brads, 1¼ " long 16 shelf bracket pins
1 x 2	17 ' clear pine 1 x 2, cut into: 4 cleats, 11⅛ " long 2 side facings, 47½ " long 2 end facings, cut to fit (about 29 ")	**Finish**	enamel undercoat and oil-based enamel
		For the jig	1 clear pine 1 x 3, 42 " long

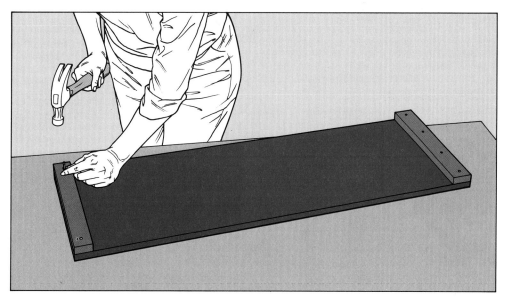

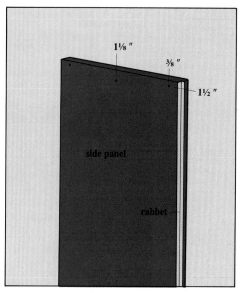

1 **Nailing cleats to end panels.** Lay an end panel on the worktable, better side down. Spread glue on the back of a cleat and align it with the end and sides of the end panel. Nail the cleat in place with three 1¼-inch brads — one near each end and one in the middle. Attach the second cleat in the same way, then attach two cleats to the other end panel.

2 **Preparing the side panels.** Following the technique in Step 1 on page 96, mark and drill three screw holes at each end of both side panels. Locate two of the holes ⅜ inch from the end and 1½ inches from each side, and center the third hole 1⅛ inches from the end. Cut a ⅜-inch rabbet along the back edge of each panel as you did for the cabinet *(page 96, Step 2)*.

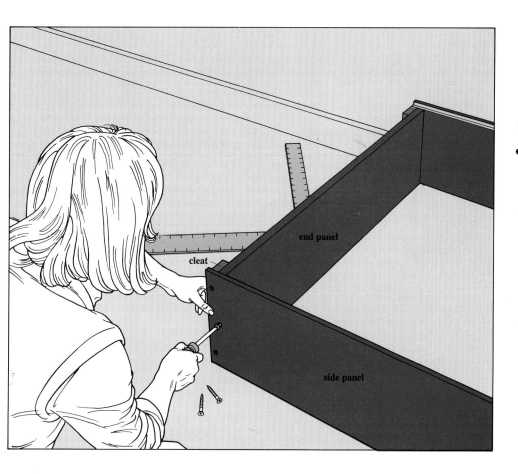

3 **Completing the frame.** Hold an end panel on the floor with one long edge upward, one end braced against the wall. Set a side panel, rabbeted edge upward, against the end panel at right angles; align the end of the side panel with the top of the cleat. Check the angle with a carpenter's square. Use a ³⁄₃₂-inch bit to drill a hole through the center screw hole in the side panel into the end panel; drive in a 1½-inch No. 8 screw *(left)*. Check the angle again. Drill through the top and bottom screw holes and drive the screws. Position the side panel against the wall and attach the second side panel to the end panel in the same way. Then install the other end panel between the side panels. Following the technique shown in Step 7, page 31, make a drilling jig 42 inches long. Follow Steps 8 and 9, pages 88-89, to complete the bookcase frame. ▶

Lighting a display

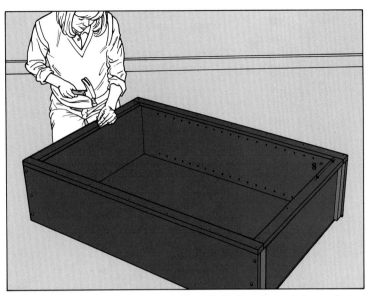

4 **Attaching facing.** Lay the assembly on its back and spread glue on the front edges of the side panels. Position each side facing so that its outer edge is even with the outer surface of the side panel. Nail the facings in place with 1¼-inch brads at 8-inch intervals. Cut upper and lower facings to fit between the side facings. Apply glue to the front edges of. the end panels and the cleats. Lay each facing in place, aligning the inside edges with the inside surfaces of the end panels. Nail the upper and lower facings in place as you did the side facings. Attach parting bead to the front edges of the shelves as you did to the lower-unit top *(page 97, Step 7)*, and finish the bookcase as described on page 94.

5 **Connecting the modules.** Place the lower unit in its permanent location. Set the upper unit on the lower unit, aligning their backs and sides. Wrap tape around a ³⁄₃₂-inch twist bit, 1½ inches from the tip, to mark the drilling depth. From inside the lower unit, drill through each hole in the top — made in Step 7, page 97 — into the upper unit until the tape marker touches the wood. Drive 1½-inch No. 8 wood screws into the holes *(above)*.

S ubstituting glass shelves for wood and concealing two slim light fixtures inside transforms the bookcase on page 100 into a display case that will show off collectibles and curios to best advantage. The shelves and lights are installed after the top and bottom units have been assembled and finished with oil, varnish or enamel.

Choose the fixtures ahead of time: The two-inch side facings on the case are wide enough to hide a variety of incandescent or fluorescent strip-light fixtures. Those here enclose tiny bulbs within a rectangular metal housing that measures slightly more than ½ inch by ½ inch and is 30 inches long. Along the back of the housing is a strip of adhesive that sticks snugly to any flat surface. Fixtures of other styles are installed with brackets or screws. The plug of this fixture snaps off so that you can thread the cord through holes drilled in the units. If the style you buy has a conventional plug, simply snip it off, thread the cord and replace it with a clamp-on plug, which you can buy at any hardware store. If you wish to have fixtures wider than ¾ inch, use 1-by-3s as facings; they will hide fixtures up to 1½ inches wide.

Clear glass shelves ¼ inch thick allow even lighting throughout the case. Tempered glass, which is nearly three times as expensive, crumbles into blunter shards when broken; but the extra safety factor is rarely necessary in this type of installation. Acrylic plastic ⅜ inch thick provides a sturdy alternative to glass, but it scratches easily and clouds with age.

Order the shelves cut ¼ inch shorter than the inside width of the case, narrow enough to clear the light fixtures by ¼ inch and with all the edges polished smooth or beveled. Support them on metal bracket pins, cushioning the glass with self-stick felt pads.

Before installing the lights and shelves, stack the upper and lower units in their final location and screw them together *(Step 5, below left)*.

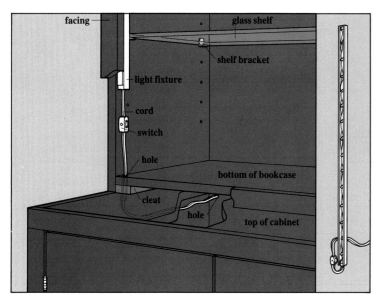

facing
glass shelf
shelf bracket
light fixture
cord
switch
hole
bottom of bookcase
cleat
hole
top of cabinet

A lighted display case. Glass shelves, ¼ inch thick and cut to fit the standard-size bookcase on page 100, measure 10¼ inches by 30¼ inches. Felt-padded metal bracket pins support them securely and are easily moved to adjust the shelves' height. On each side of the unit, a light fixture *(inset)* is mounted out of sight on the back surface of the side facing, which also hides the ON / OFF switch. With its detachable plug removed, the power cord for each fixture passes down through a hole drilled in the upper bookcase unit and the lower cabinet unit, then back through a second hole in the back panel of the lower unit. With the plug reattached, the fixture connects to a wall outlet.

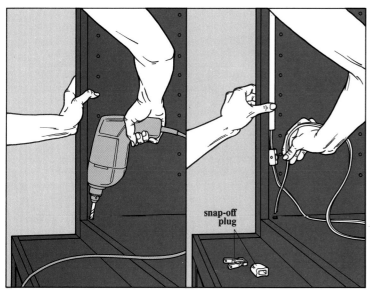

snap-off plug

Installing the light fixtures. Fit a power drill with a ¼-inch twist bit. Place the tip of the bit at a bottom front corner of the upper unit, ½ inch from the side and ½ inch from the facing. Tilting the drill at a slight angle for easier access, drill through the bottom and the cleat of the bookcase unit and the top of the cabinet unit *(above, left)*. Pull both modules away from the wall. Then, from inside the lower unit, drill through the back panel, about 1 inch from the rear upper corner. Install the fixture on the back of the facing, using the adhesive or hardware provided by the manufacturer. Remove the snap-off plug, thread the electric cord through the holes *(above, right)* and reattach the plug. Install the second fixture on the back of the opposite side in the same way.

An entertainment center

The modular units described in the previous section can be modified to house a home entertainment center. The cabinets shown below with their optional bookcases accommodate a television set, a stereo receiver, video and audio tape decks and a compact-disc player. One of the cabinets has a record bin for albums; another contains two partitioned drawers for compact-disc recordings and both audio and video cassettes.

These cabinets are variations of the base module presented on pages 95-99.

Build a basic 32-inch-wide cabinet first, then use the materials listed opposite and the instructions that follow to adapt it for a television set. The stereo cabinets are only 24 inches wide. All the materials you need for one of them are listed on page 107; materials for a 24-inch-wide bookcase are listed on page 111.

The key elements in the television cabinet are a lazy susan-style turntable and two heavy-duty metal shelf slides. Assembled with two plywood panels, they make a slide-out, rotating shelf for a 19-inch television set. The turntable and

slides can be ordered through mail-order specialty houses or your hardware store.

The turntable shown here is installed using common wood screws and machine screws. If the one you order is a different design, follow the manufacturer's instructions. The slides are made to support heavy objects and are often sold specifically as television shelf slides.

After completing the units, put your TV set and components on the shelves and mark the locations of their power cords and interconnecting cables on the cabinets' back panels. Then remove the

components and use a drill fitted with a 1-inch spade bit to bore holes for the wires. Finish the cabinets *(page 94)*.

The television cabinet must be fastened to the wall so it will not tip over when the loaded shelf is pulled out. This involves reinforcing the cabinet's back with screws, fixing a cleat to the wall, then screwing the back panel to the cleat — all of which is explained on page 110, along with instructions for fastening neighboring modules together so that the cabinets form a single structure against the wall.

A Sliding, Rotating Base for Television

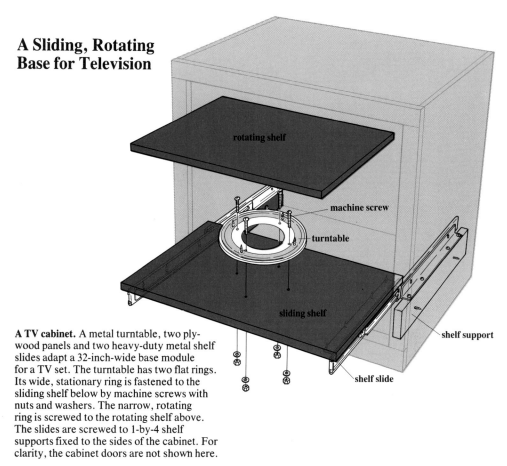

Materials List (for TV shelf)

Plywood	A2-quality ¾ " birch plywood, 4 ' x 4 ', cut into: 1 sliding shelf, 28 " x 17 " 1 rotating shelf, 24 " x 17 "
1 x 4	2 clear pine 1 x 4 shelf supports, 19⅝ " long
Hardware	1 lazy susan-style metal turntable, 12 " in diameter, 5⁄16 " thick 2 heavy-duty metal shelf slides, 18 " long 4 3⁄16 " round-head machine screws, 1½ " long 8 No. 6 round-head wood screws, ⅝ " long 12 No. 8 round-head wood screws, 1½ " long

A TV cabinet. A metal turntable, two plywood panels and two heavy-duty metal shelf slides adapt a 32-inch-wide base module for a TV set. The turntable has two flat rings. Its wide, stationary ring is fastened to the sliding shelf below by machine screws with nuts and washers. The narrow, rotating ring is screwed to the rotating shelf above. The slides are screwed to 1-by-4 shelf supports fixed to the sides of the cabinet. For clarity, the cabinet doors are not shown here.

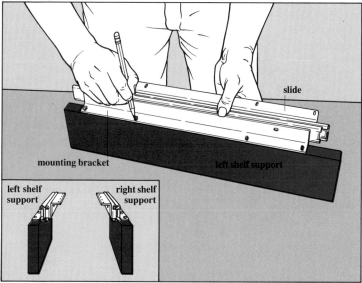

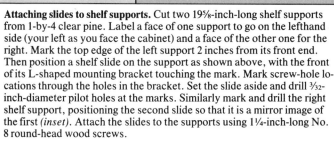

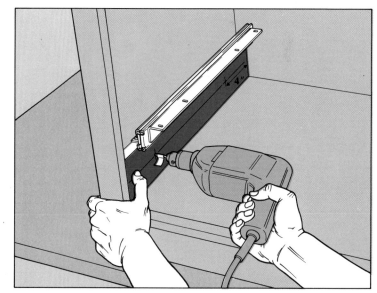

1 **Attaching slides to shelf supports.** Cut two 19⅝-inch-long shelf supports from 1-by-4 clear pine. Label a face of one support to go on the lefthand side (your left as you face the cabinet) and a face of the other one for the right. Mark the top edge of the left support 2 inches from its front end. Then position a shelf slide on the support as shown above, with the front of its L-shaped mounting bracket touching the mark. Mark screw-hole locations through the holes in the bracket. Set the slide aside and drill 3⁄32-inch-diameter pilot holes at the marks. Similarly mark and drill the right shelf support, positioning the second slide so that it is a mirror image of the first *(inset)*. Attach the slides to the supports using 1¼-inch-long No. 8 round-head wood screws.

2 **Attaching the shelf supports.** Draw a lengthwise center line on the inner face of each shelf support. Mark the lines 4 inches from each end. Lay the supports on scrap wood and drill 3⁄16-inch-diameter holes through them at the marked locations. Then fit the drill with a 3⁄32-inch twist bit and wrap tape around the bit 1⅜ inches from its tip. Set the left shelf support in the cabinet against the left side. Bore ⅝-inch-deep pilot holes in the side of the cabinet by drilling through the holes in the support *(above)*, stopping when the tape reaches the support's surface. Remove the support, apply wood glue to its outside surface and fasten it to the side of the cabinet with 1¼-inch-long No. 8 round-head wood screws. Attach the right support to the right side of the cabinet the same way. ▶

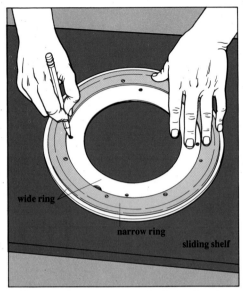

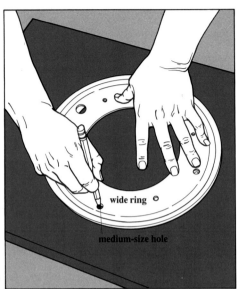

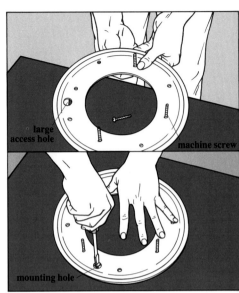

3 **Drilling turntable mounting holes.** Lay the sliding shelf — a 28-by-17-inch piece of ¾-inch plywood — on the work surface. By measuring, center the turntable on the board with the wide ring *(white)* next to the board, narrow ring *(gray)* on top. Then mark the board through the four visible small holes in the wide ring. Remove the turntable, place scrap wood under the shelf and use a drill with a ¼-inch twist bit to bore holes all the way through the shelf at the marks.

4 **Drilling the rotating shelf.** Lay the 24-by-17-inch rotating shelf on the work surface, Grade 2 side up. By measuring, center the turntable on it with the narrow ring down. Rotate the wide ring until the four medium-size holes nearest its outer edge are lined up over the four smallest holes in the narrow ring. Mark the board through the holes. Remove the turntable and use a drill with a tape-collared ³⁄₃₂-inch twist bit to bore ⅝-inch-deep pilot holes at the marks.

5 **Mounting the turntable.** With the wide ring up *(top)*, insert 1½-inch-long ³⁄₁₆-inch round-head machine screws up through its four small holes. Turn the ring so its large access hole is over a small mounting hole in the narrow ring and position both holes over a pilot hole in the rotating shelf. Drive a ⅝-inch No. 6 round-head wood screw there *(bottom)*. Pivoting the turntable and rotating the wide ring as necessary, drive screws through the other small mounting holes.

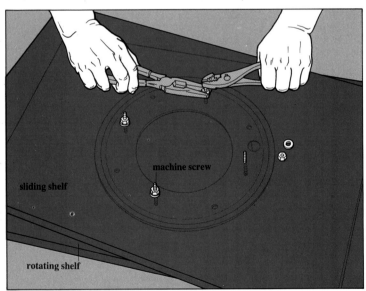

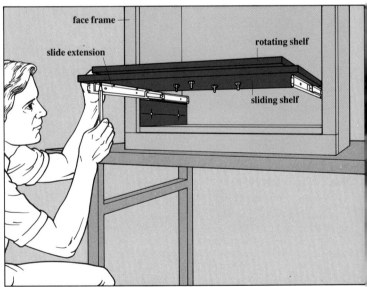

6 **Attaching the sliding shelf.** Lower the sliding shelf, Grade 2 side up, onto the turntable, fitting the ¼-inch holes in the shelf over the machine screws. Slip a ³⁄₁₆-inch washer and nut over the end of each screw in turn and, gripping the end of the screw with a pair of pliers, tighten the nut with a second pair of pliers or a small wrench.

7 **Mounting the turntable assembly.** Push the cabinet's metal slide extensions all the way in. Place the turntable assembly in the cabinet with the sliding shelf on the slide extensions. Center the shelf in the cabinet with the front edge of the shelf resting just behind the face frame. Then carefully draw out the turntable assembly on the slide extensions. Mark screw-hole locations on the underside of the sliding shelf through the holes in the extensions. Remove the shelf assembly and use a ³⁄₃₂-inch twist bit wrapped with tape ⅝ inch from its tip to bore ⅝-inch-deep pilot holes in the sliding shelf at the marked locations. Reposition the shelf assembly on the slide extensions and fasten it with ⅝-inch-long No. 8 round-head wood screws.

Housing for Components

These stereo modules are 24-inch-wide versions of the cabinet on pages 95-99. The drawers are mounted on 18-inch-long full-extension slides with elongated mounting holes for adjusting their position. (If your slides differ, follow the manufacturer's installation instructions.)

The materials listed below are for the cabinet with drawers. The other cabinet does not require the items designated for the drawers, but it will need a 1-by-2 cut to size as a stop for the record bin. The exact dimensions of the drawer pieces are determined during construction.

Materials List (one cabinet)

Plywood	1 sheet A2-quality ¾″ birch plywood, 4′ x 8′, cut into: 1 top, 23″ x 20″; 1 bottom, 22½″ x 19⅝″; 2 sides, 31¼″ x 20″; 1 adjustable shelf, 22¼″ x 19″; 1 stationary shelf, 22½″ x 19″; 2 shelf supports, 19⅝″ x 13″ A2-quality ¼″ birch plywood back, 23⅛″ x 28¾″
Lumber	12′ clear pine 1 x 3, cut into: 2 top supports, 22½″; 1 front rail, 22½″; 1 lower facing, 24″; 2 cleats, 18⅞″ 8′ clear pine 1 x 2, cut into: 2 side facings, cut to fit (about 28″); 1 upper facing, 24″ 7′ of ½″ x ¾″ parting bead, cut into: 2 top edges, 20″; 1 stationary-shelf edge, 22½″; 1 adjustable-shelf edge, 22¼″
Hardware	14 No. 8 flat-head wood screws, 1½″ long; ½ lb. fourpenny finishing nails; 1 oz. 16-gauge brads, 1¼″ long; 1 oz. 16-gauge brads, ¾″ long; 4 bracket pins
Finish	sealer and oil-based enamel
For the drawers **Plywood**	¾″ A2 birch plywood, cut into: 2 sides, 6″ x 18″; 2 sides, 4″ x 18″; 1 front and 1 back 6″ wide, cut to fit (about 18″); 1 front and 1 back 4″ wide, cut to fit (about 18″); partition, 5″ wide, cut to fit (about 16½″); 1 face piece, 8″ x 20¾″; 1 face piece, 6½″ x 20¾″ ¼″ A2 birch plywood bottom, cut to fit (about 18″ x 19½″)
Lath	1¾″ lath, 8′ long, cut to fit
Hardware	1 pair 18″ full-extension drawer slides; 4 wood handles, 3″ long; 40 No. 6 flat-head wood screws, ¾″ long; 16 No. 6 flat-head wood screws, ½″ long

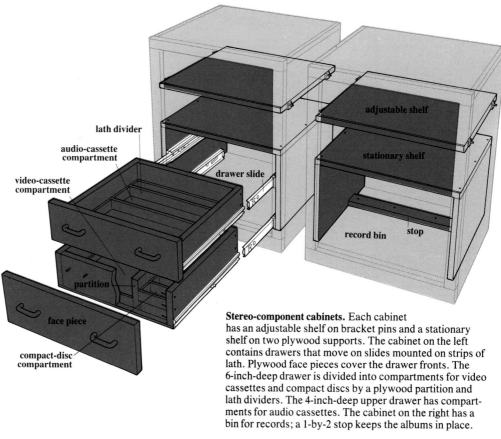

Stereo-component cabinets. Each cabinet has an adjustable shelf on bracket pins and a stationary shelf on two plywood supports. The cabinet on the left contains drawers that move on slides mounted on strips of lath. Plywood face pieces cover the drawer fronts. The 6-inch-deep drawer is divided into compartments for video cassettes and compact discs by a plywood partition and lath dividers. The 4-inch-deep upper drawer has compartments for audio cassettes. The cabinet on the right has a bin for records; a 1-by-2 stop keeps the albums in place.

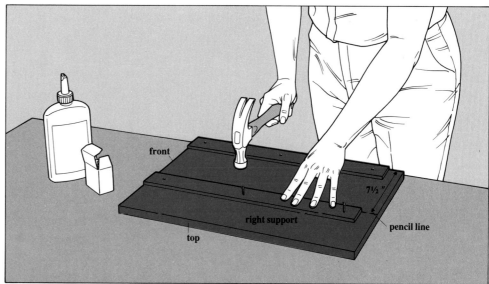

1 **Attaching lath slide mounts.** Position two shelf supports — 19⅝-by-13-inch pieces of plywood — inside the cabinet; stand them on long edges against the walls. Label the supports to indicate whether they are to your right or left, and mark their front and top edges. Remove one of the supports, lay it inner surface up on the worktable and draw a line 7½ inches from its bottom edge. Cut two strips of lath 18 inches long and start three ¾-inch-long brads evenly spaced along the center line of each one. Apply glue to the back of one strip, align it with the bottom and front edges of the support, and drive in the brads. Glue and nail a second strip so its lower edge is aligned with the horizontal pencil line. Attach a pair of lath strips to the other shelf support the same way. ▶

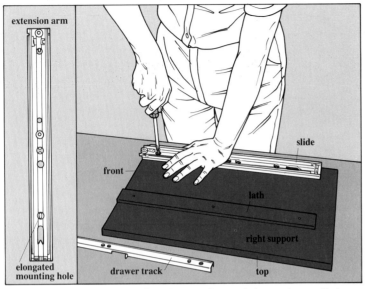

extension arm

slide

front

lath

right support

drawer track

top

elongated mounting hole

2 **Positioning the slides.** Follow the manufacturer's instructions to distinguish right- and left-hand slides, then remove the drawer track from a right-hand slide. Position the slide on the right shelf support's bottom lath, aligning the slide front with the lath front. Move the slide extension arm (light gray) to expose the two elongated mounting holes beneath it (inset) and use an awl to punch starter holes through each mounting hole. Fasten the slide to the lath with ½-inch No. 6 wood screws, then replace the drawer track. Mount the other right-hand slide and the two left-hand slides similarly. Apply glue to the backs of the supports, fit them into the cabinet and nail them with 1¼-inch brads spaced 3 inches apart along the front and back edges.

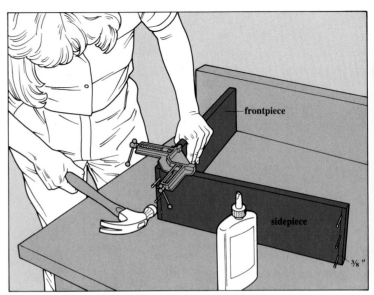

frontpiece

sidepiece

⅜"

3 **Assembling drawer frames.** Measure across the cabinet between the drawer tracks. Then measure the thickness of the plywood being used for the drawers, double it and subtract the total (about 1½ inches) from the distance between the tracks. Cut two pieces of 6-inch-wide plywood to that length (about 18 inches); these will be the drawer's front and back pieces. Start three evenly spaced fourpenny finishing nails ⅜ inch from each end of the 6-inch-wide sidepieces. Apply glue to an end edge of the drawer front and butt it against a sidepiece to form a corner. Clamp the joint and drive in the nails (above). Next, attach the drawer back to the other end of the sidepiece, then the second sidepiece to the free ends of the drawer front and back, to form a rectangular frame.

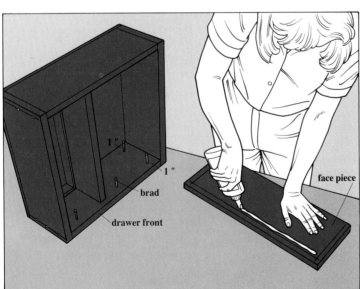

1"

1"

brad

drawer front

face piece

6 **Attaching the face piece.** Start three 1¼-inch brads into the inner surface of the drawer front, spacing them evenly 1 inch from the top edge; start three more brads 1 inch from the bottom edge. Center the drawer front on top of the 20¾-by-7-inch drawer face and mark the edges of the front on the ends of the face piece. Then remove the drawer and draw a line ⅞ inch from and parallel to the bottom of the drawer face. Apply three beads of glue ¼ inch, 3 inches and 5½ inches above the line, parallel to the long edge (above). Position the drawer with its front down and centered on the face piece, and drive in the nails. Cut a 20¾-by-5⅜-inch face piece for the 4-inch drawer and attach it the same way.

spacer

spacer

divider

divider

2"

7 **Installing compact-disc dividers.** Above the lath strips, measure the width of the narrow compartment created in Step 5 and cut eight lath strips to that length (about 5⅝ inches). Then cut 12 lath spacers 2 inches long. Glue one of the longer strips to the front and one to the back of the drawer, their lower edges resting on the strips installed in Step 5. Now, atop the strips next to the drawer's front, glue one spacer to the sidepiece and one to the partition. Put glue on the ends of a longer strip and insert it across the compartment, the ends of its lower edge resting on the lath below (inset). Repeat this sequence five times to make six more cells. Then measure between the last divider and the back of the drawer, cut two final spacers to that length and glue them in place.

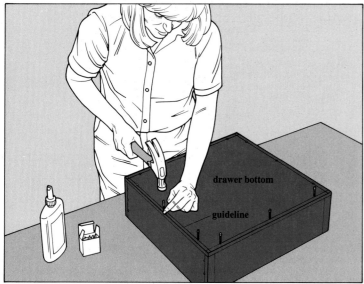

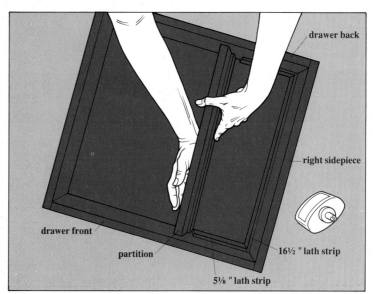

4 **Attaching drawer bottoms.** Find the outside dimensions of the drawer frame (approximately 18 by 19½ inches) and cut a drawer bottom to fit from a piece of ¼-inch plywood. Draw guidelines parallel to and ⅜ inch from each edge of the piece, then start 1¼-inch brads into the wood, spacing three brads evenly along each line. Put the drawer frame on the work surface and apply glue to its exposed edges. Place the drawer bottom on the frame and skew the frame until one corner is perfectly square under a corner of the bottom, then drive in the nails.

Using 4-inch-wide plywood, repeat Step 3 and this step to make a second drawer that is 4 inches deep.

5 **Installing the drawer partition.** Measure between the front and back inside surfaces of the 6-inch-deep drawer and cut a 5-inch-wide piece of plywood and two pieces of lath to that length (approximately 16½ inches). Glue one of the strips onto the right sidepiece, with the lath strip's lower edge on the drawer's bottom. Cut two 5⅛-inch-long lath strips and glue them to the front and back of the drawer, with their ends butted against the long lath strip. Glue the second 16½-inch lath to the plywood partition, aligning the lower edges of the two pieces. Then set the partition inside the drawer with the lath butting the ends of the two 5⅛-inch pieces *(above)*. Drive three fourpenny finishing nails through the drawer front and back into the ends of the partition.

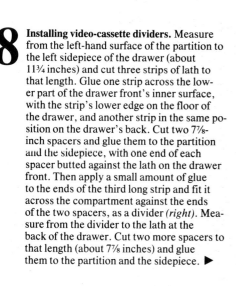

8 **Installing video-cassette dividers.** Measure from the left-hand surface of the partition to the left sidepiece of the drawer (about 11¾ inches) and cut three strips of lath to that length. Glue one strip across the lower part of the drawer front's inner surface, with the strip's lower edge on the floor of the drawer, and another strip in the same position on the drawer's back. Cut two 7⅞-inch spacers and glue them to the partition and the sidepiece, with one end of each spacer butted against the lath on the drawer front. Then apply a small amount of glue to the ends of the third long strip and fit it across the compartment against the ends of the two spacers, as a divider *(right)*. Measure from the divider to the lath at the back of the drawer. Cut two more spacers to that length (about 7⅞ inches) and glue them to the partition and the sidepiece. ▶

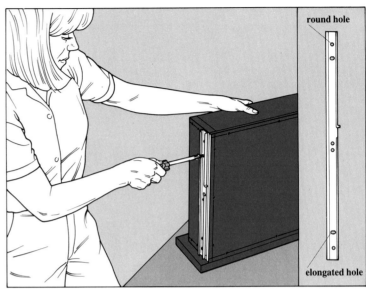

9 **Installing audio-cassette dividers.** Place the 4-inch drawer on the work surface. Measure between the right and left sidepieces and cut five lath strips to that length (about 18 inches). Glue one strip on edge at the bottom of the front and one at the bottom of the back of the drawer. Then cut six 4⅝-inch-long lath spacers. Using the longer strips as dividers, glue them and the spacers in the drawer — as you did in Step 8 — to form three 4⅝-inch-wide compartments *(above)*. Finally, measure between the face of the last 18-inch divider and the back of the drawer, cut two spacers to that length and glue them in place.

10 **Attaching drawer tracks.** Draw a line ¹¹⁄₁₆ inch from the bottom of each drawer on the outside of each sidepiece. Position the drawer track from the corresponding slide on each sidepiece, with its front end against the face piece and the elongated mounting holes centered over the line. Use an awl to punch starter holes through the mounting holes, then drive in ½-inch-long No. 6 flat-head screws. Slide the drawers into the cabinet and check their fit. If necessary, loosen the screws to shift the slides and tracks, then re-tighten them. Next, drill ¹⁄₁₆-inch pilot holes ⅝ inch deep through all the round mounting holes in the tracks and slides; drive ¾-inch-long No. 6 flat-head screws into them.

Installing and Completing the Units

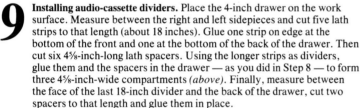

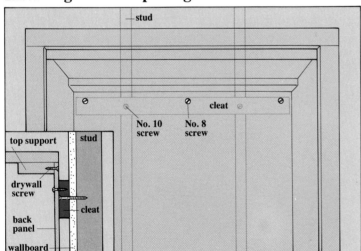

Securing the TV cabinet. Drill four evenly spaced ³⁄₃₂-inch-diameter holes through the TV cabinet back into the top support and drive 1¼-inch No. 8 drywall screws into them. Cut a 30-inch-long cleat the same thickness as the wall's base molding and at least 1¾ inches wide. With its top edge 30 inches above the floor, fasten it to studs *(page 21)* with No. 10 screws that will extend 1½ inches into the wall (2¼-inch screws are used above). Use other appropriate fasteners *(page 125)* where there are no studs. Next, drill three evenly spaced ³⁄₁₆-inch-diameter shank holes through the cabinet's back panel 29 inches from the floor. Push the cabinet against the wall and drill ³⁄₃₂-inch-diameter pilot holes through the shank holes into the cleat. Fasten the cabinet to the cleat with 1-inch-long No. 8 round-head screws.

Joining units. Drill four ³⁄₁₆-inch shank holes through the left-hand side panel of each cabinet that will abut another cabinet on that side; space the holes 3 inches from the top of the panels, 5 inches from the bottom, and 2 inches from the front and back. Push the units together. Drilling through the shank holes, bore ³⁄₃₂-inch pilot holes ⅝ inch deep into the neighboring units *(above)*. Join the modules with No. 8 screws; use 1¼-inch screws at the top, 2-inch screws at the bottom. Attach the hinged doors to the TV cabinet and install the adjustable shelves in the stereo modules with bracket pins. Finally, mount two handles *(page 99, Step 10)* on the front of each drawer, using 2-inch-long machine screws of a diameter to fit the handles, and one or more washers as necessary under the screwheads to make the handles fit tight.

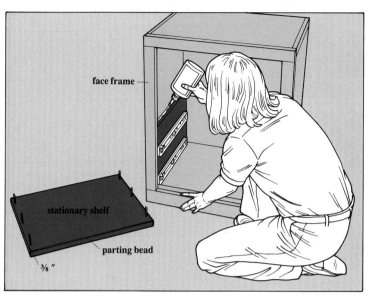

11 **Installing the stationary shelf.** Face the front of each shelf with parting bead *(page 97, Step 7)*. Start three evenly spaced fourpenny finishing nails in a row ⅜ inch from each side edge of a shelf. Apply glue to the top edges of the shelf supports, position the shelf on them, its front edge butted against the inside of the face frame, and drive in the nails. Then follow Step 7 on page 31 to make a 13-inch-long 1-by-3 drilling jig with holes spaced 5, 6 and 7 inches from the bottom. Using the jig and a drill fitted with a ¼-inch twist bit taped 1¼ inches from the tip, bore ½-inch-deep holes for the adjustable shelf bracket pins in the sides of the cabinet.

12 **Making a cabinet with record bin.** After building a second 24-inch-wide cabinet, install two 19⅝-by-13-inch shelf supports in it, as at the end of Step 2, but do not attach lath or drawer slides. Measure between the two inside surfaces of the supports and cut a 1-by-2 to that length (about 20½ inches) to serve as a stop. Apply glue to one face of the stop, and position it glued face down on the cabinet floor 13 inches back from the inside surface of the face frame. Secure it with four evenly spaced 1¼-inch brads. Finally, glue and nail a 22½-by-18-inch stationary shelf on top of the shelf supports, then drill holes for shelf bracket pins, as in the preceding step.

Modifying an Upper Unit

The 24-inch-wide bookcase units on top of the stereo cabinets on page 104 are optional; if you decide to include them as part of a wall system, you must also construct a particleboard platform like the one at right to provide a level surface on which to place your record turntable.

All of the pieces you need to build the bookcase and the platform are specified in the Materials List below. To construct the bookcase, follow the steps on pages 100-102 for building a 32-inch-wide bookcase, adjusting the measurements accordingly.

The caption at bottom right tells how the platform is put together. Spackle its surfaces and sand with medium (100-grit) sandpaper before painting it.

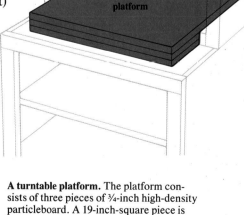

A turntable platform. The platform consists of three pieces of ¾-inch high-density particleboard. A 19-inch-square piece is supported by the bookcase's bottom shelf and two 7-by-19-inch rectangles. One of these is fixed to the square's bottom by glue and four 1¼-inch brads; the other is attached to the bottom of the first similarly.

Materials List (for one bookcase)

Plywood	1 sheet A2-quality ¾″ birch plywood, cut into: 2 sides, 11½″ x 47½″ 2 ends, 11⅛″ x 22½″ 4 shelves, 10½″ x 22¼″ 1 piece A2-quality ¼″ birch, plywood, 23⅛″ x 46″, for back
1 x 2	16′ clear pine 1 x 2, cut into: 4 cleats, 11⅛″ long 2 side facings, 47½″ long 2 end facings, cut to fit (about 21″)
Parting bead	9′ parting bead, ½″ x ¾″, cut into 4 shelf edges, 22¼″ long

Hardware	12 No. 8 flat-head wood screws, 1½″ long 16-gauge brads, 1¼″ long 16 shelf bracket pins

For turntable platform

Particle-board	¾″ high-density particleboard, cut into: 1 upper shelf, 19″ x 19″ 2 supports, 7″ x 19″
Finish	sealer and oil-based enamel

A compact home office

Framed by the modular units presented on previous pages, a recessed desk and a small bookcase above it create a cozy but efficient alcove that neatly punctuates the wall system in which it is incorporated. The low platform that holds the heavier components of a personal computer *(left)* is detachable, so the desk can be cleared for other uses, as it is on page 93. A sliding shelf comes out of hiding from beneath the desk to hold the keyboard. When not in use, the keyboard may be kept in a cubbyhole below the platform; a similar recess to the right houses printer paper.

To provide a smooth, finished look — as well as a convenient handgrip for the sliding shelf — 1-by-2 facing strips are nailed to the front edges of both the desk and the shelf. The facing strips must be carefully aligned so they do not impede the shelf's movement. Waxing the top of the shelf, the underside of the desk top and the L-shaped runners that guide the shelf will help it to slide easily.

The low platform furnishes a surface 16 inches deep and 36 inches wide. Measure your own computer components to be sure they will fit into a work station this size. If necessary, modify the dimensions of the pieces *(see the Materials List and top drawing, opposite)*.

The platform and its three vertical supports, for example, can range from 10 to 20 inches in depth (front to back); for the sake of structural integrity, the platform's width (side to side) should not exceed 40 inches. (If you are building an overhead bookcase, remember that its side-to-side dimension must match that of the desk.) The platform supports must be cut to allow at least ¼ inch of clearance above the stowed-away keyboard; measure your keyboard's height to see if the 2¾ inches allowed here is sufficient.

This platform is designed to be level with the tops of the base units on both sides; a higher platform — one made to house a thicker keyboard than the model at left — will extend above its neighboring base units unless you mount the desk top at a lower level. The desk-top position shown here puts the keyboard at a comfortable 27 inches off the floor.

Instructions for constructing the desk begin opposite; those for the upper bookcase appear on pages 118-119.

An Extendible Desk

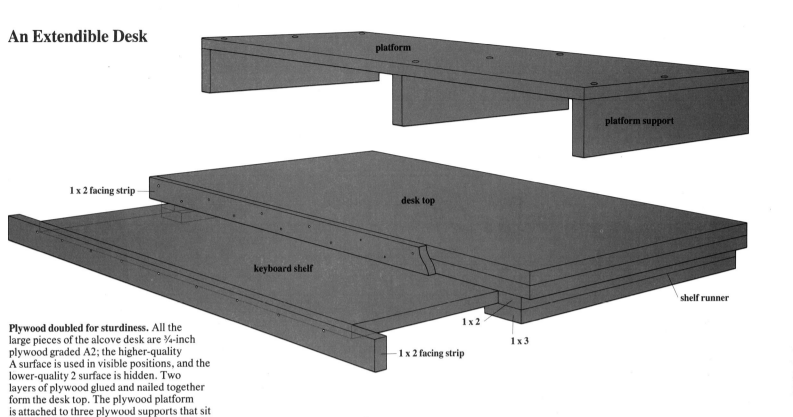

platform

platform support

1 x 2 facing strip

desk top

keyboard shelf

shelf runner

1 x 2

1 x 3

1 x 2 facing strip

Plywood doubled for sturdiness. All the large pieces of the alcove desk are ¾-inch plywood graded A2; the higher-quality A surface is used in visible positions, and the lower-quality 2 surface is hidden. Two layers of plywood glued and nailed together form the desk top. The plywood platform is attached to three plywood supports that sit unanchored on the desk top so the whole platform can be easily removed, transforming the computer station into a writing desk. The keyboard shelf slides in and out beneath the desk on L-shaped runners made from 1-by-2s nailed to 1-by-3s. The desk is mounted on 1-by-2 cleats screwed to the sides of two flanking wall modules.

Materials List

Plywood	1 sheet A2-quality ¾ " birch plywood, 4 ' x 8 ', cut into: 2 desk-top panels, 36 " x 20 " 1 platform, 36 " x 16 " 1 sliding shelf, 31⅛ " x 20 " 3 platform supports, 16 " x 2¾ "
1 x 3	42 " clear pine 1 x 3, cut into 2 shelf-runner bottoms, 20 " long
1 x 2	13 ' clear pine 1 x 2, cut into: 2 facing strips, 36 " long 2 shelf-runner tops, 20 " long 2 mounting cleats, 20 " long
Fasteners	1 oz. 16-gauge brads, 1¼ " long ¼ lb. fourpenny finishing nails 6 No. 10 round-head wood screws, 2½ " long 8 No. 10 flat-head wood screws, 2 " long 8 No. 10 flat-head wood screws, 1¼ " long 9 No. 8 flat-head wood screws, 1½ " long
Finish	sealer and oil-based enamel

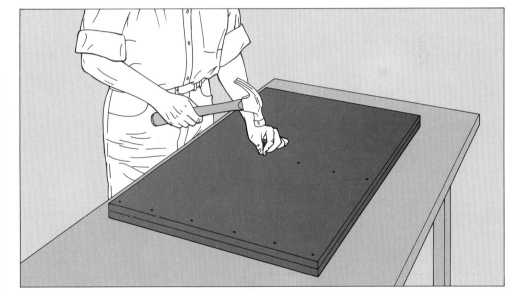

1 **Forming the desk top.** Stack one 36-by-20-inch plywood panel on top of the other and align their edges; if any edge protrudes, sand it down until the two panels match. Lay one of the panels on a smooth work surface with its Grade A side facing down (pad the work surface if necessary to protect that side of the panel, which will be the top of the desk). Squeeze parallel lines of wood glue 3 inches apart on the upper surface. Lay the second panel, its Grade A surface facing up, on top of the first. Align their edges and nail the two panels together with three rows of 1¼-inch-long brads driven at 4-inch intervals (above). With a damp cloth, wipe away any glue that seeps from between the panels. ▶

113

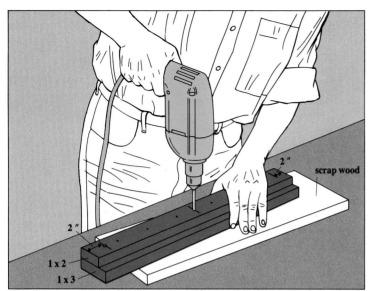

2 **Making the shelf runners.** Squeeze a line of glue down one wide face of a 20-inch 1-by-3, ¾ inch from an edge. Lay a 20-inch 1-by-2 on the glue, aligning the boards' edges on that side and at the ends to form an L-shaped runner for the keyboard shelf. Nail the 1-by-2 to the 1-by-3 with 1¼-inch brads driven at intervals of 3 to 4 inches. Carefully wipe away any glue seepage. After the glue dries, sand the inside of the L with medium (100-grit) paper, then apply furniture paste wax to the sanded surfaces and let it dry — about 30 minutes. Make another runner the same way. Now place one runner at a time on a piece of scrap wood and drill ¼-inch holes all the way through, roughly along the center line of the 1-by-2; position the holes at the middle and 2 inches from each end.

3 **Attaching the runners.** Wrap masking tape 2½ inches from the tip of a ⅛-inch bit and fit the bit into the drill. On the bottom of the desk top — the side with the nailheads — pencil a line ⅞ inch from a 20-inch edge. Align the outer edge of a runner with this line, the 1-by-3 uppermost; align the ends of the runner with the front and back edges of the desk top. Slipping the bit through the holes in the runner, drill 1-inch-deep pilot holes into the desk, stopping when the tape reaches the surface of the 1-by-3. Set the runner aside. Squeeze a line of wood glue on the desk bottom between each pair of pilot holes. Reposition the runner and fasten it to the desk with 2½-inch No. 10 round-head wood screws. Attach the other runner. Wax the bottom of the desk between runners.

5 **Attaching facing to the shelf.** Test the shelf for fit by inserting it, A side up, between the runners and sliding it in and out several times. Remove the shelf; if necessary for a looser fit, sand down the sides and the bottom (Grade 2) surface. Next, make a pencil mark 2⅜ inches from each end of the second facing strip. Start a row of fourpenny finishing nails in the strip between the marks at 4-inch intervals and ⅜ inch from one long edge.

Squeeze a line of glue down the center of the shelf's front edge. Lay the 1-by-2 on the glue, aligning one long edge with the top (Grade A) surface of the shelf so that the started nails are aimed into the shelf's front edge; center the facing strip using the pencil marks. Drive the nails. Stain or paint the top of the shelf and its side edges, then apply furniture paste wax to the top.

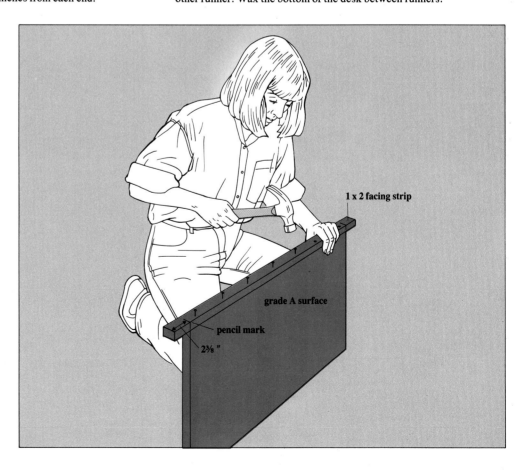

114

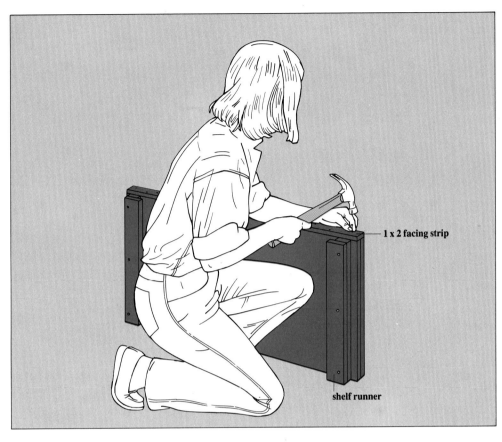

1 x 2 facing strip

shelf runner

4 **Attaching facing to the desk top.** Apply two long glue lines along the front edge of the layered desk top, one line in the center of the edge of each plywood panel. Lay a 36-inch-long 1-by-2 facing strip on the glue, aligning one of its long edges with the bottom surface of the desk top's bottom panel and its ends with the side edges of the desk. Nail the strip to the desk's front edge *(left)* with two staggered rows of fourpenny finishing nails, each row ³⁄₈ inch from an edge of the 1-by-2. If the 1-by-2 projects above the desk top's upper surface, sand the facing strip's edge down with coarse (60-grit) paper wrapped around an unpadded block of wood; to avoid marring the desk top, switch to medium (100-grit), then fine (150-grit) sandpaper as the facing-strip edge is brought flush with the surface.

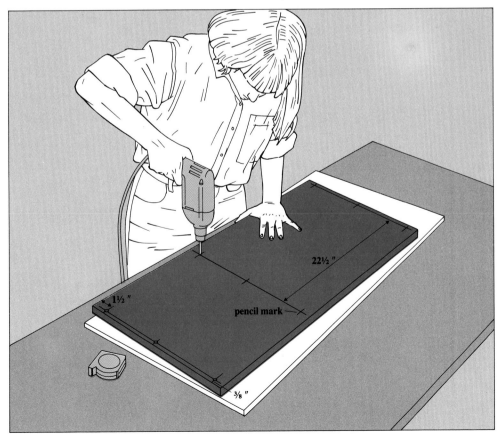

22½ "

1½ "

pencil mark

³⁄₈ "

6 **Drilling the platform.** Across the A surface of the plywood panel for the platform, use a straightedge and pencil to draw a front-to-back line parallel to and ³⁄₈ inch from each side edge. Draw a third parallel line at a distance from one side edge that is 3 inches greater than the total width of your keyboard. (The keyboard in this case is 19½ inches wide, so the line has been drawn 22½ inches from the far side edge of the 36-inch-long panel in this picture.)

Next, pencil three marks across each line — one at the midpoint, the others 1½ inches from the long (front and back) edges of the panel. Place the panel on a piece of scrap wood. Using a tape collar as described in Step 3, drill a hole ³⁄₈ inch in diameter and ¼ inch deep at each mark. Then use a ³⁄₁₆-inch bit to drill through the panel in the middle of each hole, thus creating counterbored shank holes for the screws that will fasten the platform to its supports. ▶

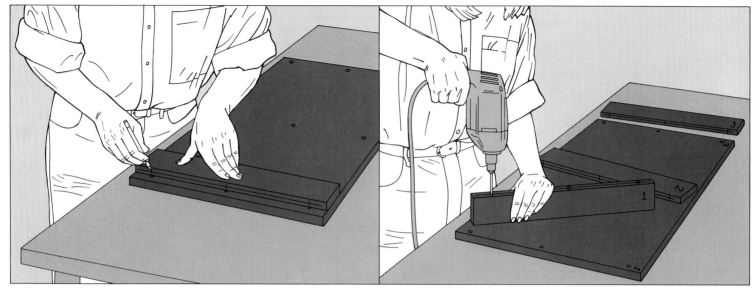

7 **Marking and drilling platform supports.** From ¾-inch-thick plywood, cut three platform supports to a length that equals the front-to-back measurement of the platform and to a width — here, 2¾ inches — that is ¼ inch greater than the height of your keyboard. Using a straightedge, draw a line down the exact center of one long edge of each support. Flip the platform panel over so that its Grade 2 surface faces upward. Lay a support flat on the panel, aligning its center-lined edge with a row of shank holes, the ends of the support flush with the front and back edges of the panel. Label an end of the support and the same end of the corresponding row of holes in the panel with the number 1 in order to pair

them again later. Pencil a mark aligned with the exact center of each hole across the center line on the support's edge *(above, left)*. Position and mark the other two supports, numbering them and their corresponding rows of holes 2 and 3. With a ³⁄₃₂-inch tape-collared bit, drill a ¾-inch-deep pilot hole in the supports at each mark *(above, right)*.

10 **Marking pilot holes for mounting cleats.** Label a long edge of each cleat to be the upper edge. Holding a cleat with its front end ¾ inch back from a base module's face, align its upper edge with the lower pencil line. With an awl, mark through the holes in the cleat to indicate pilot-hole locations on the side of the module *(above)*. Using the other cleat, mark pilot-hole positions on the other base unit. Set the cleats next to their respective cabinets. With a tape-collared ⅛-inch bit, drill a ⅝-inch-deep pilot hole at each awl mark.

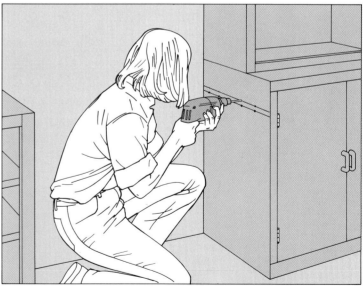

11 **Drilling upper shank holes.** Fit the drill with a ¼-inch bit. Directly above each pilot hole you made in Step 10, drill a shank hole clear through the module's side at the upper pencil line *(above)*. Now reposition the cleat as before, its labeled upper edge aligned with the lower pencil line, and attach it to the side of the cabinet with 1¼-inch-long No. 10 flat-head wood screws. Drill shank holes through the other cabinet and attach the second cleat.

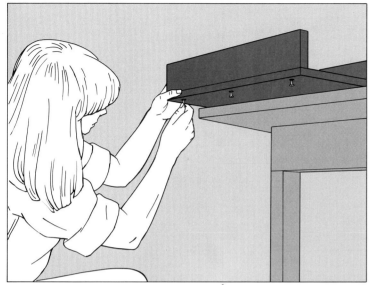

8 **Attaching the platform supports.** Apply a thin line of glue to the drilled edge of the first support. Press the support against its corresponding row of shank holes, matching reference numerals; the outer face of the support must be flush with the end of the platform. Before the glue sets, slide the end of the platform and its attached support just over an end of the table. Slip a 1½-inch-long No. 8 flat-head wood screw through one of the three shank holes, gently wiggle it until it catches in its pilot hole, and hand-turn it two or three times. Start screws in the other two shank holes, then drive all three screws home to anchor the support. Glue and screw the other two supports the same way, matching reference numerals each time. Plug the holes over the screwheads with wood putty.

9 **Marking mounting guidelines.** Along the center line of each mounting cleat, drill ¼-inch shank holes with ⅜-inch counterbore holes 2 inches and 5 inches from each end. Put the platform on the desk top. Measure from the platform's top to the bottom surface of the desk; do not include the runners. (Caution: If the platform supports are much higher than the 2¾ inches specified here, use 5 inches instead of this measurement. It will set the platform higher than the adjoining base cabinets but will keep the keyboard shelf a comfortable 27 inches off the floor.) On the side of a base module, mark this distance from the top at three points *(above)*, then draw a line connecting the marks. Draw another line ⅜ inch above the first. Mark identical lines on the side of the other base module.

12 **Mounting the desk.** Position the two modules at a distance from each other that equals the width of the desk. Lower the desk top (minus shelf and platform) into place on the two cleats. Align the front edges of desk top and cabinet and get help to push them together for a snug fit. Using a ⅛-inch bit taped 2 inches from the tip, drill from inside a cabinet through the shank holes made in Step 11, boring 1¼ inches deep into the end of the desk. Drive 2-inch-long No. 10 flat-head wood screws into the holes. Check the alignment of the other end of the desk top, drill pilot holes and fasten it with screws the same way. After covering visible screwheads and filling the plywood edges with spackle, sand and paint the desk top and platform. Finally, put the shelf and platform in place.

Making a Case for Books

Bridging the gap between upper flanking bookcases with a smaller one encloses the desk shown on page 112 in a snug niche and affords the user ready access to reference materials. Basically, the bookcase is built the same way as the upper modular unit described on pages 100-102, so review those steps before starting. The difference — as is shown in the drawing below and the steps opposite — is that this bookcase, because its bottom is visible, has an extra plywood panel covering its underside in place of two unsightly cleats.

The height of the bookcase — 24¾ inches — is roughly half that of the upper modules on either side, and its front-to-back measurement, 11½ inches, is the same as theirs so the fronts will be flush. Its width, of course, must be identical to the width of the desk top — here, 36 inches — to fit precisely into the space between the flanking units. The Materials

List at right is based on these dimensions. For a bookcase of a different size, check the drawing below against the Materials List and adjust the figure for every component that is affected by the change. (For instance, to make the bookcase 2 inches wider, add 2 inches to the long, side-to-side dimension of the top, the shelf, the bottom, the bottom finishing panel, the back, and the top and bottom facing strips.)

Because of its considerable bulk and weight (about 35 pounds), the bookcase is installed by means of a stratagem (Step 3) that requires lifting it only once. For this you will need two pieces of 1-by-3 or other strong scrap wood, each about 3½ feet long, to use as temporary supports. Once in place above the desk, the bookcase is anchored by screws driven into its sides from inside the neighboring upper modules.

Materials List	
Plywood	1 sheet A2-quality ¾ " birch plywood, cut into: 2 sides, 11½ " x 24 "; 1 top and 1 bottom, both 11⅛ " x 34½ "; 1 bottom finishing panel, 11½ " x 36 "; 1 shelf, 10½ " x 34¼ " A2-quality ¼ " birch plywood, cut into 1 back, 24 " x 35 "
1 x 2	12 ' clear pine 1 x 2, cut into: 2 cleats, 11⅛ " long; 1 top and 1 bottom facing strip, each 36 " long; 2 side facing strips, cut to fit (about 21 ")
Parting bead	1 shelf-edge strip, 34¼ " long
Hardware	12 No. 8 flat-head wood screws, 1½ " long; 12 No. 8 round-head wood screws, 1¼ " long; fourpenny finishing nails; 16-gauge brads, 1¼ " long; 4 shelf bracket pins
Finish	sealer and oil-based enamel

A bookcase accompaniment. This scaled-down version of a modular bookcase resembles its full-size cousin (page 100). The frame and shelf are made from ¾-inch plywood, the back from ¼-inch plywood; the adjustable shelf is trimmed with parting bead. The frame is reinforced by 1-by-2 cleats at the top, and 1-by-2 facing strips touch up the front edges. Because the underside can be seen, it is given a neatly finished look by an extra plywood panel that covers the bottom, hiding the lower edges of the sides and back and eliminating the need for cleats to brace the bottom corners. At the rear of the bookcase, the lower edge of the back sits on the rabbet-like lip of this bottom finishing panel.

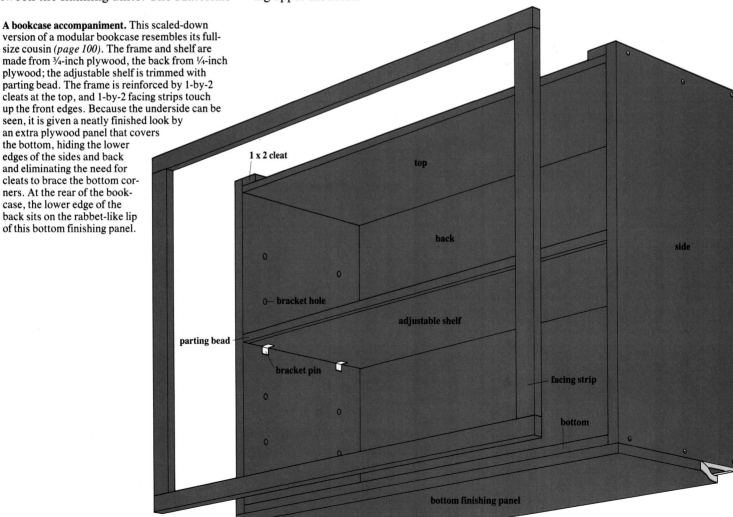

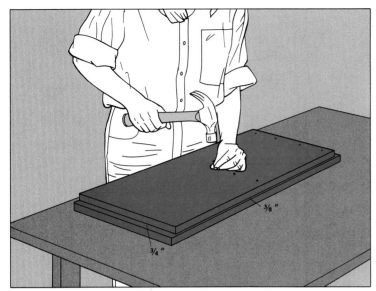

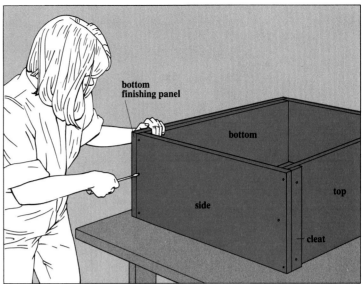

1 **Joining the lower panels.** Lay the bottom finishing panel, Grade 2 surface up, on a worktable. Draw a pencil line ¾ inch from and parallel to each end. Over the area between those lines, squeeze parallel beads of wood glue spaced at intervals of about 2 inches. Then lay the bottom piece, with its Grade 2 surface facing down, on the glue, aligning the panels' long edges on one side and aligning the ends of the shorter panel with the pencil lines on the longer one. Now drive three rows of 1¼-inch brads through the shorter panel and into the panel below.

2 **Building the case.** Construct the bookcase according to instructions in Steps 1 through 4 on pages 100-102, with the following exceptions:
● Attach cleats to the top panel only, not the bottom panel.
● When drilling screw holes near the lower end of each side panel, do not stagger them; position all three in a uniform row ⅜ inch from the end.
● Set the side panels into the rabbet-like Ls formed by the bottom and the bottom finishing panel; then drive screws to fasten sides to the bottom (*above*); set the back into the L at the rear of the bottom.
● Start the holes in the drilling jig 4½ inches from the top end, so the adjustable-shelf holes will be aligned with those of flanking units.
● Attach top and bottom facings first, then cut side facings to fit.

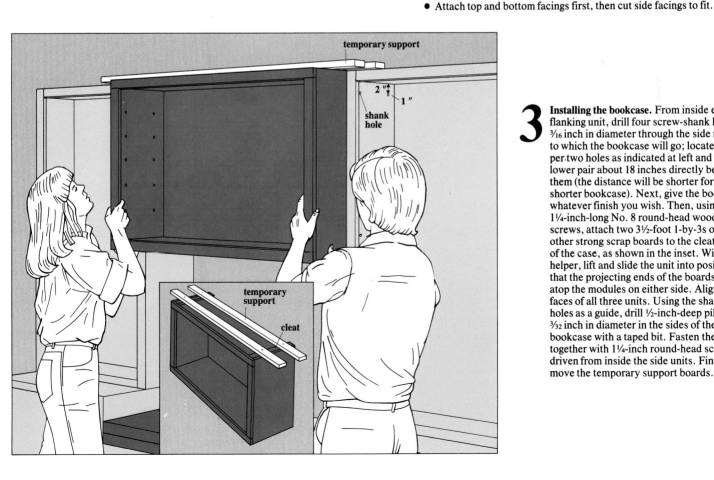

3 **Installing the bookcase.** From inside each flanking unit, drill four screw-shank holes ³⁄₁₆ inch in diameter through the side next to which the bookcase will go; locate the upper two holes as indicated at left and the lower pair about 18 inches directly below them (the distance will be shorter for a shorter bookcase). Next, give the bookcase whatever finish you wish. Then, using 1¼-inch-long No. 8 round-head wood screws, attach two 3½-foot 1-by-3s or other strong scrap boards to the cleats on top of the case, as shown in the inset. With a helper, lift and slide the unit into position so that the projecting ends of the boards rest atop the modules on either side. Align the faces of all three units. Using the shank holes as a guide, drill ½-inch-deep pilot holes ³⁄₃₂ inch in diameter in the sides of the bookcase with a taped bit. Fasten the units together with 1¼-inch round-head screws driven from inside the side units. Finally, remove the temporary support boards.

Using power tools safely and efficiently

Power tools ranging from saber saws to variable-speed drills are indispensable aids to a home decorator who is making and installing shelves, bookcases and modular wall cabinets. If purchased wisely and handled properly, the tools on these pages will ensure swift and slick results even for the novice.

In general, inferior tools produce inferior work no matter how experienced the user may be. When looking for shop tools, pass by the least expensive ones. At hardware stores, many lumberyards and home-improvement centers, you should be able to find tools of medium to high quality at moderate prices.

Look especially for such features as heavy-duty electrical cords, permanently lubricated bearings that simplify tool maintenance, and double-insulated plastic bodies that eliminate the need for a grounded power cord with a three-prong plug. Cordless power drills can be used everywhere and, like standard electric drills, can accommodate a full spectrum of accessories, including screwdriving, sanding and polishing gear.

Just as important as buying the right tools is using the right tool for the job. A saber saw, for example, is designed for cutting curves *(below)*. Although a saber saw also can make a long, straight cut through plywood, the cut will be cleaner and more precise if it is done with a circular saw *(opposite)* or table saw *(pages 122-123)*. For tricky angle cuts and maximum precision, a table saw is best.

All power tools come with manufacturer's instructions for care and handling. Take the time to read them, then practice with the tools before you begin a project.

Safety is as important as skill in the operation of power tools, and a few rules apply in every situation:
● Dress for the job. Avoid overly loose clothing, tuck in your shirt and roll up your sleeves. Tie back your hair if it is long. And wear goggles when there is a possibility that dust or shavings will fly into your eyes — for example, whenever you are cutting with a circular saw or a table saw or when you are drilling at eye level or overhead. However, do not wear gloves when operating power tools; gloves reduce dexterity and can catch in moving parts.
● When operating a power tool, be sure to work on a stable surface; with wood projects, clamp materials to the surface whenever practical.
● Stand comfortably, do not reach any farther than you easily can and never position yourself directly in front of — or directly behind — a moving saw.
● When making long cuts in boards or plywood, recruit a helper to support the work. Circular saws tend to kick back toward the operator if the blade gets jammed in the middle of a cut; this generally happens when the sawed section has not been properly supported. If the blade binds while you are making a cut, switch the saw off immediately and support the work to open the cut.
● Always unplug power tools when they are not in use and whenever you make an adjustment or change parts.

The Saber Saw

Because the narrow blades of a saber saw are only about ¼ inch wide, they can be maneuvered through tight spots and intricate, curved cuts without binding or breaking. With straight cuts, the narrow blade tends to wander from a guideline. Choose a wider ⅜-inch or ½-inch blade and clamp a straightedge guide to the work *(opposite, bottom)* to keep such cuts on line.

Your best buy is a variable-speed saw that you can speed up along broad curves and slow down for tricky areas. Blades are sold individually or in sets. Depending on their length, they will cut through wood up to 4 inches thick. Blades with five or six teeth per inch usually make fast, rough cuts; blades with 10 to 14 teeth per inch cut more slowly, but also more cleanly. For fine cuts in plywood, buy taper-ground blades with 10 teeth per inch.

To ensure a smooth cut on the good face of a board or panel, work with that surface down. The saber-saw blade cuts on the upstroke, sometimes tearing slivers from the top surface of the work.

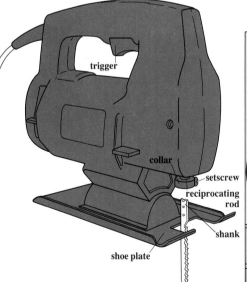

A variable-speed saber saw. A trigger in the handle lets you turn the saw on and off and regulate the speed with which it cuts. To insert a blade, loosen the setscrew in the collar on the reciprocating rod with a screwdriver or a hex wrench, depending on the saw model. Push the blade's notched shank as far as it will go up into the hollow portion of the reciprocating rod, then retighten the setscrew to anchor the blade.

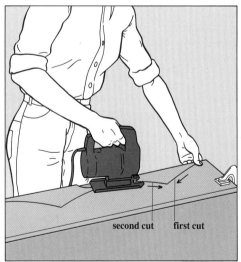

Cutting a curved pattern. Plan cuts so as not to force the blade through an impossibly tight turn; here, both cuts move toward a sharp corner. Rest the tip of the shoe plate on the wood. Start the saw, and guide the blade into the wood, swinging the back of the saw right or left as you move into curves. Do not force the blade, lest it bind or break. If you end a cut with the blade in the wood, let the blade stop before withdrawing it.

The Circular Saw

The easiest way to get wood cut to size is to have it sawed at a lumberyard. To avoid this extra expense, however, you may decide to cut the pieces yourself. For woodwork, trim and boards up to a nominal 1-by-4 in size, you can make precision cuts quickly with a miter box and a sharp backsaw *(page 31, Step 8)*. For larger boards and plywood panels, you may want a circular saw *(right)* or table saw *(overleaf)*.

Which to use depends on how exact your cuts must be. The inexpensive, portable circular saw, though designed for rough carpentry, will cut the pieces for many projects with reasonable accuracy. More demanding jobs — such as those calling for close-fitting joints — require a table saw.

The standard circular saw for home use has a 7¼-inch blade that will cut through lumber up to 2 inches thick; for bevels, it tilts to any angle from 45° to 90°. To saw without binding, the motor should develop at least 1½ horsepower.

A variety of blades *(top)* is available for different cutting tasks. Carbide-tipped blades, although more expensive, will outlast ordinary steel blades and save money in the long run.

In operating the saw, a firm grip is extremely important. A 7¼-inch model weighs about 10 pounds and seems heavier at arm's length, when you are cutting large panels. For added safety, buy a saw that has two handles to grip.

A circular saw can be guided freehand for short cuts; for longer cuts, clamp a guide to the workpiece for accuracy *(right)*. The manufactured edge of ¼-inch plywood makes a good, straight guide. Always support lumber from below; without support, the board or panel may crack. Work the saw so that its heavy motor passes over the guide if you are using one.

Many accessories for circular saws are available at hardware stores. One patented metal guide can replace the wood straightedge shown at right; another simplifies rip cutting. A circular-saw table, which holds the saw underneath it upside down, offers the stability and accuracy of the table saw at a lower price, with some loss of versatility.

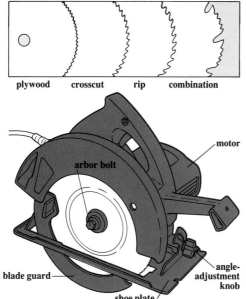

plywood   crosscut   rip   combination

The saw. Driven by a powerful motor, the blade of a circular saw cuts on the upstroke. A spring-activated guard, which slides up into the housing of the saw during operation, drops back down over the blade as the cut is finished. The angle-adjustment knob lets the shoe plate be tilted for beveled cuts. The arbor bolt, which holds the blade in place, unscrews so the blade can be changed.

Blade styles. A fine-toothed plywood blade slices through plywood without splintering it. A crosscut blade's small teeth tear smoothly across the grain; a ripping blade's larger teeth, set at a sharper angle, saw with the grain. A combination blade both rips and crosscuts, with small teeth separated by deep indentations.

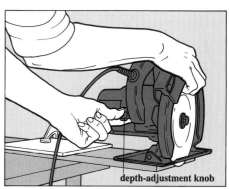

Adjusting blade depth. With the saw unplugged, loosen the depth-adjustment knob at the back. Lay the shoe plate flat on the wood and push up the blade guard. With one hand, hold up the guard while grasping the blade housing to support the saw. Keeping the shoe plate flat, raise or lower the saw until the blade is about ¼ inch below the bottom of the board to be cut. Retighten the depth-adjustment knob.

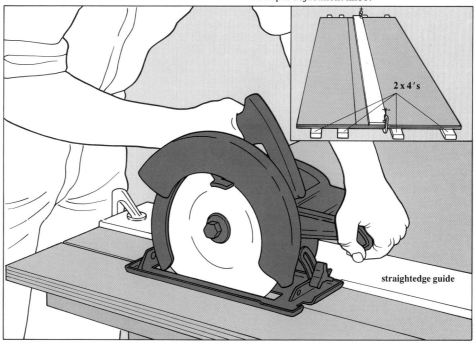

Sawing with a straightedge. Clamp a straightedge to the board to be cut so the blade falls just on the waste side of the cutting line. Put on goggles before sawing. To cut a large plywood panel *(inset)*, rest the panel on the floor, on 2-by-4s. Holding the saw firmly, cut slowly along the straightedge. Do not force the blade — it may bind. Keep a steady grip on the saw as it clears the board, and prepare to catch its unsupported weight.

The High-Speed Router

Spinning razor-sharp bits at 25,000 rpm — or faster — routers make quick work of carving out joints and shaping contours in wood and plastic laminate. The motor, which should be at least ¾ horsepower for home use, is mounted vertically on a two-handled base that is flat at top and bottom. A collet at the bottom of the motor shaft secures the bit. The secret of router safety is to grip the tool firmly and move it steadily: Pushed too fast it loses speed and chews out big bites; pushed slowly, the bit scrapes at wood and tends to bounce off the cut.

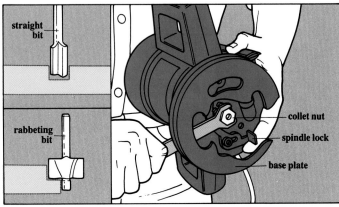

1 **Installing a bit.** Be certain the router is unplugged. Then, for this model, reach underneath the base plate and pull the tab of the spindle lock with your fingers; the spindle lock will engage the spindle and hold it in place. Loosen the collet nut by turning it counterclockwise with a collet wrench. For cutting a dado joint, insert a straight bit *(top inset)* into the collet as far as it will go and retighten the nut. For a rabbet joint, use a rabbeting bit *(bottom inset).*

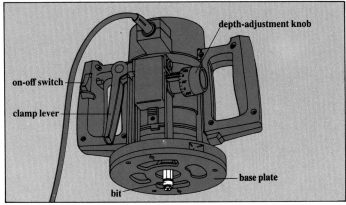

2 **Adjusting the cutting depth.** With the router unplugged, swing the clamp lever on this model to the unlocked position. Turn the depth-adjustment knob, which raises and lowers the motor and bit in relation to the base plate, and relock the clamp lever. For making joints, you can adjust the router so that the cutting edge of a bit extends any distance from its full length to only a fraction of an inch beyond the base plate.

The Table Saw

The stability of its blade and the guides built into its generous work surface make the table saw the tool professional cabinetmakers use for precision cutting. The saw's fence, an adjustable metal straightedge, slides over the table parallel to the blade and locks in place as a guide for ripping — cutting boards lengthwise. The miter gauge is used to advance wood perpendicular to the blade for crosswise cuts.

For diagonal cuts, the front face of the miter gauge guides boards at any angle set on the gauge's calibrated dial. A blade-tilting mechanism under the table swivels the blade, angling it for beveled cuts. Used in tandem, the miter-gauge dial and blade-tilting mechanism set up tricky compound-angle cuts.

Bench-top table saws — lightweight, miniaturized versions of standard table saws — are portable and suffice for cutting small pieces of wood. However, large panels need the greater table area and stability of a standard table saw.

Like circular saws, table saws are sized by the diameter of the blades they use — from 8 to 12 inches — and the same blade types are available. A typical home saw, with a 10-inch blade, can cut 3¼ inches deep.

For cutting small pieces safely, use the miter gauge or a push stick to feed the wood, and keep hands away from the blade. Never stand directly behind the blade: Wood binding in the blade can be kicked sharply backward. Always disconnect the saw before adjusting the blade.

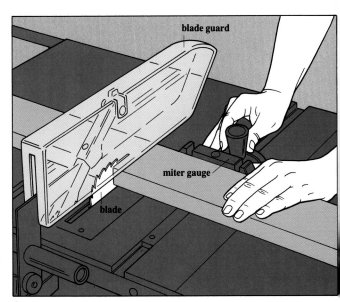

Making a crosswise cut. Slide the fence out of the way. Put on goggles; plug in the saw and lower the blade guard. Set the edge of the board against the miter gauge, then move the gauge and board forward together until the blade falls on the waste side of the cutting line but is not touching the board. Switch on the saw and cut slowly on the line and through the board, holding the board at its supported end — not the free end that is to be cut off. Turn off the saw and give the board a little sideways shift to free it from the saw blade. Remove the cut piece from the saw.

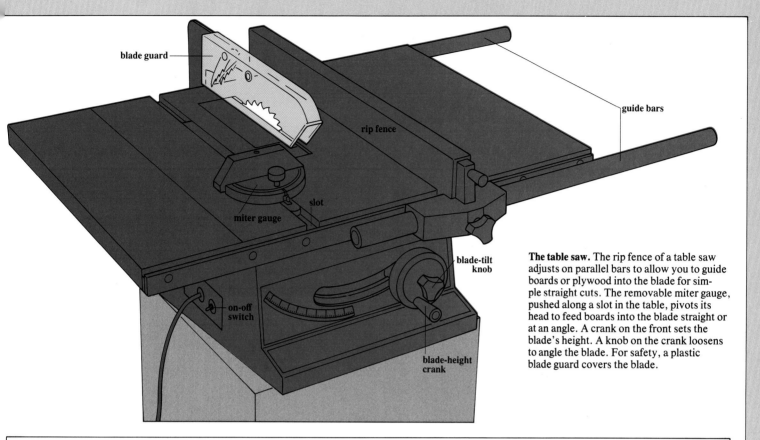

blade guard

guide bars

rip fence

slot

miter gauge

blade-tilt knob

on-off switch

blade-height crank

The table saw. The rip fence of a table saw adjusts on parallel bars to allow you to guide boards or plywood into the blade for simple straight cuts. The removable miter gauge, pushed along a slot in the table, pivots its head to feed boards into the blade straight or at an angle. A crank on the front sets the blade's height. A knob on the crank loosens to angle the blade. For safety, a plastic blade guard covers the blade.

Using the Table's Rip Fence

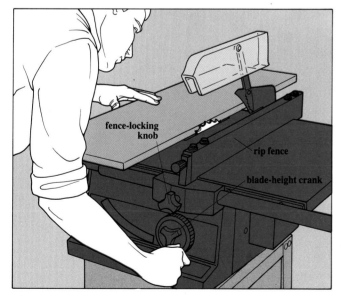

fence-locking knob

rip fence

blade-height crank

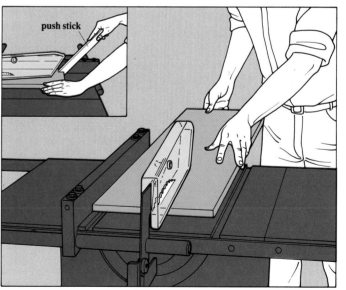

push stick

1 Setting up the table saw. Unplug the saw. To adjust the fence for the width of the cut, loosen the fence's locking knob and measure from the fence to the blade with a ruler or tape measure. Position the fence so that the saw kerf — the cut made by the blade — falls just on the waste side of the cutting line. Lock the fence. Turning the blade-height crank, raise the blade so that its teeth are just slightly higher — no more than ¼ inch — than the piece of wood to be cut.

2 Making a lengthwise cut. Put on goggles, plug in the saw and lower the blade guard. For a large piece, get a helper to support it as it passes beyond the table. Turn on the saw and press the wood against the fence, then forward into the blade. When the end nears the blade, advance the wood with a push stick (*inset*), made by sawing a corner off a wood scrap. Cut all the way through the wood and push it clear of the blade before turning off the saw.

The Variable-Speed Drill

Like the saber saw, the variable-speed drill works at different speeds, depending on how hard you squeeze its trigger. Small holes in wood are bored at the fastest speeds; slower speeds are better for drilling large holes in wood and for drilling any hole in metal or masonry.

The ⅜-inch drill at right can accommodate bit shanks from 1/64 inch to ⅜ inch in diameter. Within that range, many different bits are available to drill holes from 1/64 inch to 1½ inches in diameter. Power drills also can hold the shanks of such accessories as plain or Phillips™ screwdrivers, buffing wheels and hole saws.

In this volume, the drill is most often used to drill the hole for a wood screw that fastens together two boards. This task usually requires three holes: one in the bottom board to grip the screw's threads tightly, and two successively wider holes in the top board for the shank and head. You can use a separate twist bit for each hole, then broaden the top hole with a countersink bit. Or you can bore all three holes at once with a counterbore bit, which matches the shape of the screw's threads and shank, and has an adjustable head that countersinks, or counterbores, a recess for the

screwhead. Avoid cheap counterbore bits: They tend to clog.

Spade bits bore holes up to 1½ inches in diameter; because these bits tend to wobble, use of a drill guide is advisable. The model at right, below, will fit any drill with a threaded shaft.

Masonry bits, with closely spaced, carbide-tipped edges, grind slowly into brick and concrete, which would crumble around a twist bit.

Masonry and spade bits are most often sold singly; countersinks are sold in only one size. Counterbore and twist bits are sold singly and in sets that include the most frequently used sizes.

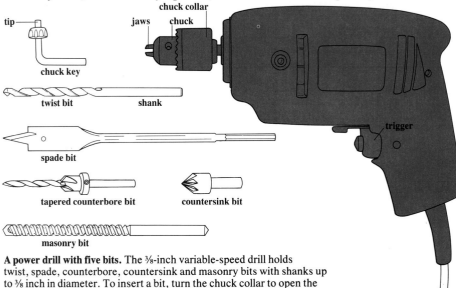

A power drill with five bits. The ⅜-inch variable-speed drill holds twist, spade, counterbore, countersink and masonry bits with shanks up to ⅜ inch in diameter. To insert a bit, turn the chuck collar to open the jaws, push the bit shank between the jaws and tighten the collar by hand until the jaws grip the shank. Then push the tip of the chuck key into one of the three holes in the chuck, and twist the key handle. To change bits, loosen the collar with the chuck key before turning it by hand.

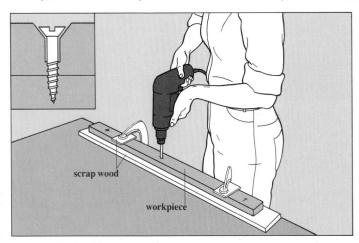

Using a power drill. Clamp the work to a table and indent the wood at the starting point with an awl. To govern a hole's depth, wrap tape around the bit at the required distance from the tip. Set the bit in the dent, squeeze the trigger and push straight down with steady, moderate pressure. To drill holes for a wood screw *(inset)*, use a tapered counterbore bit. Or drill two holes of increasing size, a narrow one in the bottom piece for the screw's threads and a wide one in the top for the shank. Widen the hole's mouth with a countersink bit if it will be puttied, or use a third twist bit if it will be plugged with a short dowel.

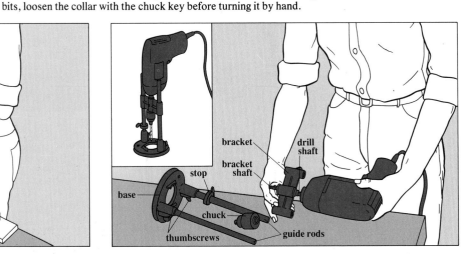

Attaching a drill guide. Remove the drill's chuck. (Most unscrew from the drill shaft, but check the manufacturer's instructions.) Twist the guide bracket onto the drill shaft; screw the chuck onto the bracket shaft. Slip the guide rods through their holes in the bracket, loosen the thumbscrews on the base, set the ends of the rods flush with the bottom of the base, and tighten the screws; this procedure ensures that drilled holes are perpendicular to the work surface when the drill guide is upright *(inset)*. If you want to drill to a certain depth, position the stop on the guide rod after you have inserted a bit in the chuck.

Appropriate Wall Fasteners

The walls of today's typical wood-frame house are skeletons of upright 2-by-4 studs spaced 16 inches apart — center to center — and covered with plaster or wallboard. When you want to attach shelves or cabinets to such walls, studs make ideal supports and wood screws *(right)* are the perfect fasteners.

But when you want to attach shelves or cabinets to the spaces between studs, you need toggle bolts or Molly® bolts, which cling to a wall by squeezing from both sides *(below, left and center)*.

Expanding anchors also are available for use with masonry walls *(far right)*, which can bear a load at any point. If the surface of a masonry wall is exposed and you have a choice, avoid joints since mortar is comparatively soft and crumbly.

In recent years the partition walls of many apartment buildings have been built with metal studs. Self-tapping screws, which have sharp threads that hold tightly in sheet metal *(below, right)*, are recommended for this type of construction.

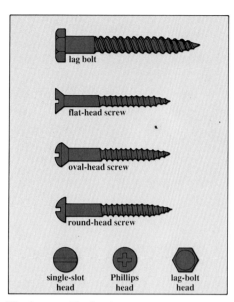

Wood screws. Flat-head screws are countersunk flush with the surface or hidden beneath plugs or putty. Round and oval heads can be left exposed. Phillips heads, with two crossed slots, are less likely to rip under turning pressure than single-slot heads. Gauge numbers denote screw-shaft diameters: The higher the number, the larger the diameter. Diameters of lag bolts, whose hexagonal *(shown)* or square heads are turned by wrenches, are expressed in inches.

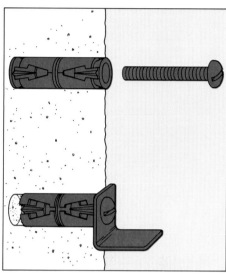

Expansion shield. This metal device with interior threads is used with a matching machine screw to hold a load on masonry or a thick plaster wall. Drill a hole that will hold the shield snugly, and tap the shield into it. Make sure the screw is long enough to extend through the object being hung and the shield. As you tighten the screw, wedges in the shield will be pulled toward the middle, pushing the cylinder sides hard against the masonry or plaster.

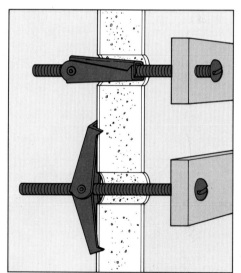

Toggle bolt. A toggle bolt must be long enough for its wings to spring open and grip the inside of a hollow wall. Drill a hole large enough for the folded wings to pass through, but do not push them in yet. Unscrew the wings from the bolt, slip the bolt through the object to be hung, and replace the wings. Then push the bolt through the wall; when the wings pop open, the bolt will feel loose. Pull the device back so that the wings will bite into the inside of the wall as you tighten the bolt.

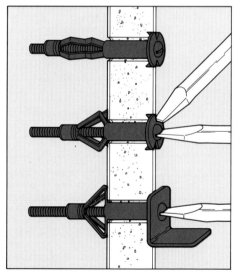

Molly bolt. The cylinder near the bolthead of this hollow-wall anchor should be as long as the wall is thick. Tap the Molly bolt into a hole drilled to its diameter. Wedge a screwdriver into one of the indentations in the flange to keep the sheath from turning as you tighten the bolt with another screwdriver. The sheath arms will splay out against the inside of the wall. Do not overtighten, or you may break the Molly bolt's arms. Remove the bolt to put the load on it, then screw it back in place.

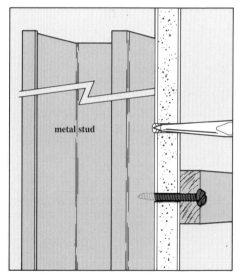

Self-tapping screw. This screw is used to attach weights to metal studs. Drill a small hole in the wallboard to the face of the stud. Make a starter dent in the stud with a center punch and a hammer. Then use a twist bit to drill a pilot hole half the diameter of the screw through the thin metal. Insert the screw through the object you are hanging, and drive it into the stud; the screw should be long enough to reach about ½ inch beyond the face of the stud.

Acknowledgments

The index for this book was prepared by Louise Hedberg. The editors are particularly indebted to the following individuals: Lynn Addison, Hyattsville, Maryland; David Bennett, Alexandria, Virginia; Skip Saunders, Outer Banks Deck Builders, Alexandria, Virginia. For their help in the prepara-tion of this volume, the editors also wish to thank: Rachelle Amato, MD Le Mobilier Composable, Paris; Bright Flowers & Ideas, Alexandria, Virginia; Giuseppe Bucalossi, SAC, Certaldo, Italy; Excalibur, Alexandria, Virginia; Walter Grazzani, Milan; Robert J. Kleinhans, Tile Council of America Inc., Princeton, New Jersey; Lewis F. Lipnick, Your Silent Partner, Arlington, Virginia; Fratelli Longhi, Meda, Milan; Franco Menna, Milan; Piero Sartogo, Rome; Studio Azzurro, Milan; S. C. White, National Hardwood Lumber Association, Memphis, Tennessee.

Picture Credits

The sources for the photographs in this book are listed below, followed by the sources for the illustrations. Credits from left to right on a single page or a two-page spread are separated by semicolons; credits from top to bottom are separated by dashes.

Photographs: Cover: Michael Latil, photographer / Luneville earthenware, courtesy Martin's, Washington, D.C., Little Caledonia, Washington, D.C., and Iberian Imports, Alexandria, Virginia. 2, 3: Guy Bouchet, photographer / design by Chaton Saconay, Paris; Tim Street-Porter, photographer, from Elizabeth Whiting and Associates, London / Arquitectonica, architects, Miami. 4, 5: Emmett Bright, photographer / Piero Sartogo, architect, Rome. 6, 7: Gianni Basso, photographer / Franco Menna, architect, Milan; Deidi Von Shaewen, photographer, Paris / Franco Bombelli, architect, Barcelona. 8: Guy Bouchet, photographer, Paris. 9: Giovanna Piemonti, photographer, Rome. 10, 11: MD Le Mobilier Composable / design by Tito Agnoli, Programme Lineal L15, Paris. 24: Georgia-Pacific Corporation. 28: Michael Latil, photographer / flowers dried and arranged by Eleanore Wall and Margaret Wall. 34: Dan Cunningham, photographer. 38: Fil Hunter, photographer. 44: Fil Hunter, photographer / toys from John Davy Toys, Alexandria, Virginia / rocking horse from The Two Harolds Antique Shop, Alexandria, Virginia; Fil Hunter, photographer / lamp, boxes from Placewares, Alexandria, Virginia / chair from Door Store of Washington, D.C. / original lithograph by Ackermann, from Gallerie Julian, Alexandria, Virginia. 45: Fil Hunter, photographer / pottery by Jane Larson / African soapstone bird from Full Circle, Alexandria, Virginia. 52: Fil Hunter, photographer / bronze sculpture by Elim Dutra, courtesy Touchstone Gallery, Washington, D.C. / "Clear Calla Fan" lamp by Joseph Sitko, courtesy The Best of Everything, Ltd., Washington, D.C. / picture frame, clock, prism, courtesy Time and Again, Washington, D.C. / tortoise-shell boxes, ivory box, ostrich eggs, courtesy Marston Luce Gallery, Washington, D.C. / glass sculpture by Robert Stephan, courtesy Jackie Chalkley, Washington, D.C. 56: Michael Latil, photographer / Turkish Kilim rug and large tree basket, courtesy Full Circle, Alexandria, Virginia. 60: John Neubauer, photographer / bookcase designed by John Brimijoin, Burtonsville, Maryland / pillow, courtesy Pierre Deux, Washington, D.C. 68: Michael Latil, photographer / Luneville earthenware, courtesy Martin's, Washington, D.C., Little Caledonia, Washington, D.C., and Iberian Imports, Alexandria, Virginia. 77: Fil Hunter, photographer. 78: John Neubauer, photographer / Levolor® blinds from Shade & Shutter Shack of Georgetown, Washington, D.C. / pillows by Kimberly Haldeman, courtesy Appalachiana, Bethesda, Maryland / women's shoes from Bradshaws, Alexandria, Virginia / men's shoes from J. C. Penney, Alexandria, Virginia / inset, John Neubauer, photographer. 84: Michael Latil, photographer. 92, 93: Michael Latil, photographer / audio and video components from Excalibur, Alexandria, Virginia / lamp, clock, desk equipment and chair from Placewares, Alexandria, Virginia / gemstones from Olde Towne Gemstones, Alexandria, Virginia. 94: Michael Latil, photographer / gemstones from Olde Towne Gemstones, Alexandria, Virginia. 104: Michael Latil, photographer / audio and video components from Excalibur, Alexandria, Virginia. 112: Michael Latil, photographer / chair from Placewares, Alexandria, Virginia.
Illustrations: 17: Artwork by Roger Essley. 19-23: Drawings by Roger Essley, inked by Frederic F. Bigio from B-C Graphics. 25-27: Drawings by Roger Essley, inked by Walter Hilmers Jr. from HJ Commercial Art. 29-33: Drawings by George Bell, inked by Frederic F. Bigio from B-C Graphics. 35-37: Drawings by George Bell, inked by John Massey. 39-43: Drawing by Fred Holz, inked by Frederic F. Bigio from B-C Graphics. 46-51: Drawings by Greg DeSantis, inked by Elsie J. Hennig. 53-55: Drawings by Roger Essley, inked by John Massey. 57-59: Drawings by Fred Holz, inked by Frederic F. Bigio from B-C Graphics. 61-67: Drawings by William J. Hennessy Jr., inked by Walter Hilmers Jr. from HJ Commercial Art. 69-75: Drawings by William J. Hennessy Jr., inked by Walter Hilmers Jr. from HJ Commercial Art. 79-83: Drawings by Fred Holz, inked by Eduino J. Pereira. 85-91: Drawings by George Bell, inked by Frederic F. Bigio from B-C Graphics. 95-102: Drawings by George Bell, inked by Stephen A. Turner. 103: Drawings by George Bell, inked by Walter Hilmers Jr. from HJ Commercial Art. 105, 106: Drawings by George Bell, inked by Walter Hilmers Jr. from HJ Commercial Art. 107-111: Drawings by George Bell, inked by Frederic F. Bigio from B-C Graphics. 113-119: Drawings by Fred Holz, inked by Arezou Katoozian Hennessy. 120, 121: Drawings by Roger Essley, inked by Adisai Hemintranont from Sai Graphis. 122, 123: Drawings by Fred Holz, inked by Frederic F. Bigio from B-C Graphics. 124: Drawings by Roger Essley, inked by Adisai Hemintranont from Sai Graphis. 125: Drawings by Fred Holz, inked by Walter Hilmers Jr. from HJ Commercial Art.

Index/Glossary

A
Accent lights, 68, 69
Adjustable shelves: in bookcase, 28-31; in bookcase module, 100; in cupboard, 84-91; made with metal tracks and bracket clips, 20; in stereo cabinet, 107, 111; on wall standards, 22-23; around window, 61, 66
Adobe construction, support rods in, 56
Alcove: accent lights for, 68, 69; building, to hold glass shelving, 68-75; glass shelf in, 34-37
Angle irons, 18, 19, 39, 42, 44, 48
Antique brass (finish), 76
Around-window bookshelves, 60-67; planning, 61; removing baseboard for, 67
Audio cassettes, storage for, 107, 110

B
Bail pulls, 76, 77
Baseboard molding, 39; removing, 67
Base cap molding, 68, 75
Bed molding, 28, 29, 32
Board lumber: buying, 16; calculating length of, 61; characteristics and qualities, 17; finish-grade, 28; grades, 16, 17; hardwood, 16, 17; softwood, 16, 17; standard sizes, 16, 17
Bookcase: building a traditional, 28-33; connecting to cabinet module, 102; modified base module, 111; in modular unit, 92-93, 94, 100-102; as part of computer unit, 112, 118-119
Books: number of, per running foot, 18; and size of shelves, 28
Bookshelves: building around window, 60-67; double-ladder, 52-55; inside-track, 38-43; ladder-supported units, 44-51; size of, 18; standards and brackets, 22-23
Bracket clips, 20
Bracket pins, 29, 31, 61, 66, 69, 75, 100, 103, 107, 111
Brackets: keyhole (for heavy loads), 23; knife, 22, 23; wood, with backplate, 23
Bracket shelf, 24-27
Bracket tracks (standards): for adjustable shelves, 20; anchoring to studs, 22; cutting, 20; for inside-track bookshelves, 38-43; on masonry, 22; mounting, 20, 22; recessed into dadoes, 20; wall shelves, 22-23
Brads, blunting point of, 47
Brick, support rods in, 56

C
Cabinets: adapted for stereo and accessories, 104, 107-111; base of modular unit, 92-93, 94, 95-99; building a country cupboard, 84-91; connecting to bookcase module, 102; hardware, 76, 77; television, 104-106; in window seat, 78; wood for, 16
Carbide-tipped bit, 124
Carbide-tipped blade (for circular saw), 121
Cassettes, video and audio, storage compartments for, 107, 109, 110
Catches, 76, 77; magnetic, 76, 95, 99
Ceiling, locating joists in, 21
Circular saw, 120, 121; blades, 121; cutting plywood, 120, 121; releasing blade, 120
Clear (grade of lumber), 17
Cleats: attaching, 97, 101, 118, 119; mounting desk on, 113, 116; supporting bracket shelf, 24, 27
Clips: bracket, 20; flush, 20; gusset, 20; joint (corner), 18, 19
Collet nut, on router, 122
Common (grade of lumber), 16, 17
Compact discs, storage compartments for, 107, 108

Computer work station: adapted from base module, 112-119; desk with slide-out shelf, 112-117
Coping saw, cutting molding with, 34, 37
Counterbore bit, 124
Countersink: *To set the head of a fastener flush with or below the wood's surface, so it can be hidden by wood putty or a wood plug.* Bit, 80, 124; technique, 80, 87
Crosscutting, 121, 122
Cupboard: attaching hardware to door, 90-91; building, 84-91
Curves, cutting with saber saw, 120

D
Dadoes: for bracket tracks, 20; cutting, 85, 86-87, 122
Desk, as part of modular system, 112-117
Display case: building, 102-103; planning, 18
Doors: attaching hardware to, 90-91; hanging onto cabinet, 99
Double-ladder shelves, 52-55; finishes for, 53; weight and size, 52-53
Dowel plugs, 24, 94
Drawers, building for base module, 107-111
Drill. *See* Variable-speed drill
Drill bits: tape-collared, 31, 105, 114; types, 124
Drill guide, 124
Drilling jig, 31
Drywall nail, removing from stud, 59

E
Edge molding, 83
Entertainment center, constructing, 104-111
Epoxy, for anchoring support rods, 56
Expansion shield, 125

F
Face frame, for cabinets, 30, 31, 85, 88-90
Fasteners, types of, 125
Filler blocks, 52, 53
Finger-jointed molding, 29, 34; painting over, 34
Finished sizes, of lumber, 16
Finishes: for molding, 34; on plywood, 94
First (grade of lumber), 16, 17
Floating shelves, 56-59; dimensions, 56; and wall construction, 56
Fluorescent strip lights, 102, 103
Full-surface hinge, 76, 77
Furring strips, 61, 65, 69, 71

G
Glass: tempered, 34, 102; weight of, 34
Glass shelves: in display unit, 102-103; in lit alcove, 68-75; supported by molding, 34-37
Grading system (of lumber), 16, 17
Grain: *In wood, ''grain'' most commonly designates the direction of the longitudinal fibers of wood tissue; it also can mean the wood's surface appearance — the pattern, arrangement or quality of the fibers.* In board lumber, 17; in plywood, 17, 78, 94
Grit number: *Sandpaper grit numbers most commonly range from 60 to 400. The higher the number, the finer the sandpaper.*

H
Hacksaw, cutting metal tracks with, 20
Handles, 76, 77
Hardware: for assembling shelf units, 19; attaching to door, 91; cabinet, 76, 77. *See also specific examples*

Hardwood: characteristics and uses, 16, 17; grades, 16, 17; plywood, 16, 17; smooth-finished, 16
Hinges: attaching, 91, 98, 99; cutting mortises for, 94, 98; full-surface, 76; piano, 78, 82; types, 76, 77

I
Inside-track shelves, 38-43

J
Jig: drilling, 31; of lath and particleboard, 44, 47, 53
Joint (corner) clips, 18, 19
Joints: cutting dadoes and rabbets, 85, 86-87, 122; rabbet, 94, 95, 96
Joists, locating, 21

K
Kerf, 94
Keyboard shelf, for computer unit, 112, 113-115
Kiln-drying: *Removing excess moisture from green wood in a kiln (oven) under controlled conditions of heat, humidity and air circulation. Kiln-dried lumber is generally preferred to that which has been dried by exposure to air;* 16

L
Ladder-supported shelf units, 44-51; dimensions, 44
Lag bolt, 125
Laminate, wood or plastic, cutting, 122
Laminated wood, building ladders of, to support shelves, 52-55
Latches, 76, 77
Lath: attaching, 39, 40, 44, 46, 49, 52, 53, 55; in drawer construction, 107, 108, 109, 110; jig made of particleboard and, 44, 47, 53
Lighting: accent lights for alcove, 68, 69; fluorescent strip lights, 102, 103

M
Machine screws, 104, 105, 106, 110, 125
Magnetic catches, 76, 95, 99
Masonry: attaching standards to, 22; drill bits, 56, 124; fasteners for, 125
Metal: bits for drilling into, 124; stud, 125
Miter box (and backsaw): cutting dowel plugs, 24; cutting molding, 31, 75, 121; using handsaw with, 39; using stopblock with, 46
Modules, wall, 92-93; adapting for television, 104-106; audio or stereo center, 107-111; building the basic unit, 94-102; computer unit, 112-119; connecting modules, 102, 110; desk, 112-117; display case, 102-103; fastening to wall, 110
Molding: baseboard, 39; base cap, 68, 75; bed, 28, 29, 32; coped, 34, 35, 37; cutting with miter box, 31, 75, 121; edge, 83; finger-jointed, 29, 34; finishing, 34; ogee cap, 28, 29, 33; parting bead, 28, 29, 30, 46, 50, 97, 100, 102, 111; quarter-round, 66; removing baseboard, 67; roman ogee cap, 34, 91; sanding, 34; screen, 79; shoe, 39, 42; staining, 34; standard lengths, 34; to support glass shelf in alcove, 34-37
Molly® bolts, 125
Mortises, cutting for hinges, 94, 95, 98
Mounting block, 48

N
Nail set, 29, 32, 33
Nominal sizes, 16, 17

127

Time-Life Books Inc. offers a wide range of fine recordings, including a *Big Bands* series. For subscription information, call 1-800-621-7026, or write TIME-LIFE MUSIC, Time & Life Building, Chicago, Illinois 60611.